Soldier *of the* Union

Private George Hechler (left) and brother Private John Hechler

Soldier *of the* Union

Private George Hechler's Civil War Service

by Ken Hechler

Pictorial Histories Publishing Company 2011

Library of Congress Control Number 2011926521

ISBN 978-157510-157-6

First Printing: April 2011

Cover Design
Amy Drake, Barboursville WV

Photos Courtesy
Jim Rogel and Tony Zeller

Typography & Book Design
Arrow Graphics, Missoula MT

Published by
Pictorial Histories Publishing Company, Inc.
1125 Central Avenue, Charleston WV 25302
Distribution center
713 South Third West, Missoula MT 59801
phone (406) 549-8488, fax (406) 728-9280
WEB pictorialhistoriespublishing.com

Contents

1. Hechler Family Leaves Germany for U.S.

GEORGE HECHLER was born in Schwaigern, Wurtemburg, Westphalia, Germany, on October 17, 1840, the son of a farmer named Gottfried Hechler and his first wife, Christine Weisenstein. Although George's mother died in Germany when he was only six years old and Gottfried remarried twice, George vividly remembers his mother and talked and wrote about her frequently. In contrast, he never mentions his father who apparently had little influence on him.

Schwaigern was formerly a walled town and encampment of the Romans. Before the Reformation it was the seat of a bishopric. A devout Lutheran, George pumped the pipe organ in the church and would sometimes climb up into the belfry for a view of the surrounding countryside.

One Hechler ancestor was a member of Napoleon's army on its ill-fated expedition to Moscow. It took him five years to find his way back to his native village. Several members of the Hechler family had the concession to carry the mail over a portion of the trade route from Nuremberg to Nancy, France.

For the most part, the Hechlers were coopers, carpenters or farmers bound to the soil. One Hechler ancestor was a glazier who spent his life repairing stained glass windows in cathedrals throughout central Europe; he kept a diary in Latin, in which, after telling of having repaired the eye of St. John on the right tower of the cathedral at Mainz, he relates a sure cure for the stomach-ache which had been confided by a fellow guild-worker at Milan.

In 1928, when my father visited Schwaigern to check up on family history, he discovered that the head of Schwaigern's prestigious Public Works Department was named "Hechler" and several others with the same name held public positions in the town.

In 1850, Gottfried's twin sister, Elisabetha, and her husband emigrated from Germany and settled in Marietta, Ohio. In 1854, wanting to join Elisabetha in Marietta, the Hechlers liquidated their property in Schwaigern and proceeded to Le Havre, France, to board a sailing vessel for New York when George was 13 years old. The trip took seven weeks. It was a stormy trip with waves as high as houses.

George Hechler's grandson, Ken, sits beside the trunk that carried all the clothes and possessions of the family—plus dried fruit and meats and provisions for baking bread on board—on their voyage to New York. The trunk is made of unfinished pine, now dark brown, of planks of varying widths, ¾ inches thick. The trunk is 22 inches tall and 43 inches long, and 22.5 inches wide. Two metal bands encircle the trunk, which is hinged. The lid is flat, and there are metal handles on either side. On the front in black lettering is: GOTTFRIED HECHLER, Le Havre N. [to] New York. The chest is presently (2011) in the possession of Jane and Wiley Pearson. Jane Pearson, born in 1948, is the great-great-granddaughter of Gottfried Hechler and his second wife, Christina Betz.

After landing on Ellis Island, they took a train West to the Ohio River, then proceeded by boat to Marietta.

Gottfried purchased a small tract of land at Harmar, a hillside suburb of Marietta in which he built a log cabin for shelter. One day while I was serving in Congress I visited the home of a Marietta lawyer named Charles Heckler, who explained he became so fed up with his clients misspelling his name that he changed it from Hechler to Heckler. One day we trampled through the woods on Harmar Hill until he found and pointed out to me the ruins and the foundation of the original log cabin which Gottfried Hechler and his sons had built with axe, cross-cut saw, hammer, nails and logs on Harmar Hill.

Early in 1861, Gottfried broke his leg, making it necessary for George and John to take over all the work on their farm. When President Lincoln called for volunteers, they both agreed they would enlist to fight for the Union, but they also made a solemn pact to stay on the farm until all the crops were harvested. Despite this pact, John climbed out the window of his room in August, 1861, descended down a well-placed ladder and sneaked away to enlist a month before George did. The two brothers wound up together in Company G of the Ohio Volunteer Infantry Regiment.

George was 5 feet, eight inches tall and weighed 135 pounds. When he enlisted, a limited number of uniform sizes were in stock; he had to remodel the shirts to keep the collars from coming up to his ears.

Kate (christened Katherine Barbara) was born November 27, 1837, a mentor for her three-year younger brother George, who adored her and was the recipient of all his letters while he was serving in the Army. Kate lived with a wealthy Ohio family named King for several years as a companion and governess for their three daughters. She went to Dalton to live with George's family in 1898; she stayed there until a few months before her death in a Kansas City hospital. She died of cancer in 1917.

John Hechler, George's younger brother by three years, born on August 10, 1843,was captured at Chickamauga and died in Andersonville prison on September 11, 1864.

Kate Hechler, 1837–1917

John Hechler's gravestone.

2. Parkersburg Divided

Town of 2,500 — Elevated to Mayor — Valuable Lifeline

THE PARKERSBURG NEWS of October 20, 1859, carried a scare headline which read: "Terrible Insurrection at Harpers Ferry." The story started: "On Monday last the whole country was electrified with the report by telegraph that a terrific insurrection had broken out at Harpers Ferry. Rumors of all kinds were flying as to participants and its cause."

Parkersburg was a divided city during the period when events were moving the nation toward the war of brother against brother. Still a part of Virginia in name and fact, many Parkersburg residents could not bear the thought of cutting their ties with the South. Yet a substantial number of citizens had pushed westward to the Ohio River in the pioneer days, and they felt a certain restlessness that the Virginia legislature did not share their advanced opinions on internal improvements, taxation and engineering work on the Ohio River. Editorially, the Parkersburg News stated on December 28, 1860: "Western Virginia, from its geographical position, must ultimately unite with the states in the Valley of the Mississippi."

IN 1860, PARKERSBURG was a lively town of 2,500, prospering from the completion of the B & O Railroad three years earlier, and the busy, partially macadamized Staunton Turnpike from the southeast and the Northwestern Turnpike from the east. Parkersburg had two lumber mills, which conditioned lumber for houses and boat-building, and also a boatyard which constructed steamboats. There were also three grist mills and four steam tanneries which procured hides from St. Louis and sent tanned leather to the eastern seaboard for sale.

The oil boom began with operations along the Hughes River in Wirt County late in 1859, and spread to Petroleum and Burning Springs before the end of 1860.

In the political arguments which boiled over secession and the Union, western Virginia vs. the tidewater, etc., slavery vs. abolition was never a dominating theme in Parkersburg. A pamphlet published in July, 1860, entitled "Notices of Parkersburg, Virginia" states:

> Let it be said to the citizens of the Free States looking for new homes, that Slavery in northwestern Virginia is an institution practically existing only in name, as the present census already shows most conclusively, the insignificant number of slaves exhibited in that of ten years ago having dwindled to a handful, while, the free blacks being few, free white labor is the productive power of the region with no drawback from the competition it meets with in people of color, elsewhere south of Pennsylvania.

ONE OF THE MANY JACKSONS whom the people of Parkersburg down through the years elevated to become their mayor was General J. J. Jackson. On January 11, 1861, General Jackson penned a sober letter to two of his Marietta friends, T. W. Ewart and C. F. Buell, which read in part as follows:

> I am in receipt of yours of the 9th, inviting me to attend the public Union Meeting in Marietta tomorrow. I am truly grateful to learn that the people of Marietta are duly impressed with the impending dangers to the country; and that you will be able to take a conciliatory and forebearing attitude. It is no time when our country is imperiled to be particular in our discussions of past shortcomings. Our true duty is to deal with the existing malady, and endeavor to discover and apply the remedy. The national distemper is highly alarming, and the remedy is entirely in the hands of the Republican Party.

Mass meetings at the Court house were frequently held in the early month of 1861 in Parkersburg, largely to rally Union sentiment. The firing on Fort Sumter burst on the city like a giant thunderclap and stimulated a flurry of early recruitment of both Union and Confederate troops to fill President Lincoln's initial call for 75,000 volunteers.

ATHWART THE RIVER, turnpike and railroad routes, Parkersburg assumed great strategic significance when the Civil War broke out. The B & O Railroad was a valuable lifeline for transportation of Union troops and supplies from the west and the Confederates, knowing this, tried and frequently succeeded in cutting the lifeline. Maj. Gen. Robert E. Lee, Commander of Virginia's armed forces, on April 29, 1861 ordered Major Alonzo Loring at Wheeling to muster into service such troops as might help protect the railroad. On May 4, 1861, General Lee ordered Col. George A. Porterfield to proceed westward from Harpers Ferry to Grafton, and to protect the railroad as well as to recruit volunteers in Wood, Wirt, Roane, Calhoun, Gilmer, Ritchie, Pleasants and Doddridge counties to assemble at Parkersburg.

General George B. McClellan was not idle, however. He dispatched troops to Parkersburg to proceed eastward toward Grafton and to protect the B & O Railroad. Locally, new rows broke out over the use of arms for home guards. A number of arms were stored in the county jail in Parkersburg and during April Union and Confederate sympathizers staged a pitched battle for their possession; finally the Union men secured the arms and used them to arm a home guard company. General McClellan arrived personally in Parkersburg on June 21, 1861 to direct operations in western Virginia. He pushed on eastward leaving another famous general, W. S. Rosecrans, in charge of the Union forces in Parkersburg.

In July, the Battle of Bull Run, routing the Union forces, was a shock to President Lincoln and the north. Recruiting was rushed. Once the crops were harvested on his hill farm at Harmar near Mar-

General George B. McClellan

ietta a 20-year old youngster named George Hechler came to Parkersburg on September 20, 1861 and signed up for a three-year hitch with the 36th Ohio Volunteer Infantry. George's younger brother John volunteered earlier in the same unit. In the heavy fighting in which both brothers were engaged, George was wounded at Antietam, and John, was captured at Chickamauga. Both George and John spent some time in Parkersburg during the Civil War. They saw the war from the combat infantry soldier's point of view.

3. Skirmishes in Roane County

Huge Meteor — Sobering News
George Enlists — Trains Surrounded — Marched 25 Miles

A FEW MINUTES AFTER NOON on the first day of May, 1860, the people of Parkersburg, Marietta and other Ohio River valley communities were startled by a loud and unearthly noise in the sky.

There was a tremendous roar like the explosion of many steamboat boilers, accompanied by the intense brilliance of a terrifying object as large and round as a full moon, trailed by a dozen times the diameter of the ball. Chunks of this huge meteor soon blackened the sky over Parkersburg, and most of the pieces fell on the Ohio side of the river. One huge stone, weighing 103 pounds, is now on display at the Marietta College Science Building.

Less than a year later, the cannon blazed at Fort Sumter on April 14, 1861. When the news reached the Ohio Valley, the sudden terrifying shock of the streaking meteor seemed strangely significant in the course of history.

TO GEORGE HECHLER, the oldest boy in a family of nine, the news was sobering. With axe and cross-cut saw, George had worked tirelessly to cut down the white oak trees, roll them, and burn or ship them down-river to Parkersburg to the lumber mills. On their hill farm a few miles outside Marietta, the heavy work fell on 21-year old George and his brother John. Frequently, George would cross the Ohio River to Williamstown or take the boat downstream to Parkersburg to buy farm implements or utensils, or earn a little extra money by working a temporary job in the oil fields east of Parkersburg.

GEORGE AND JOHN AGREED it was only a matter of time before they would join up and fight for the Union, despite the large amount of Confederate sentiment in the area. They made a solemn pact to stay home until harvest time in 1861. But one morning in early August, John did not come down for breakfast. A hasty search revealed an unslept bed—and another adventurous underage youngster had run away from home to enlist in the conflict. George followed a month later, enlisting at Parkersburg.

A contemporary letter tells of John Hechler's experiences with Co. G., 36th Ohio Volunteer Infantry, in an expedition through Wirt and Roane counties.

> At Parkersburg, we stepped aboard the railroad cars and were off—we knew not where. The train stopped at Walker's Station and we turned out to commence our first march. The route lay in a southerly direction, across the Hughes River.
>
> Here the first incident or mishap took place.
>
> Just after crossing the Hughes River, Frank Stewart accidently shot himself in the head and instantly expired (a comrade asked him to hold his gun while he adjusted his knapsack. In taking it, the locks of the two pieces came in contact, when the hammer of his own gun was thrown back with sufficient force to discharge the piece.) This melancholy turn of affairs cast a gloom over the whole column, and the remainder of our march, which terminated at Elizabeth that day, seemed more like the advance of a funeral train than the onward progress of a little army eager for a fight.
>
> At Elizabeth, we quartered in a church and Sunday morning struck out for our destination, refreshed from a sleep on the soft side of an oak board. All went well until we arrived at a stop 14 miles beyond Elizabeth, when our advanced guard of cavalry was fired into by secessionists secreted in the bushes up a hill-side, and one man mortally wounded. One company was immediately thrown out as skirmishers, and the "villainous devils" sneaked off.
>
> Nothing more of note happened during the remainder of the

CAPTAIN, LATER MAJOR JEWETT PALMER, JR.,

day and we encamped for the night at the three forks of Reedy. We were ten miles from Spencer, the county seat of Roane county, where we understood two companies of home guards were besieged by 700 secessionists. Companies of skirmishers roamed the woods on either side to prevent an ambuscade. About noon a squad of four cavalry was fired into but nothing material resulted from it with the exception of one man had his coat somewhat torn by a rifle ball.

We entered Spencer about four in the afternoon, and found it in the possession of four companies of the 4th Virginia and home guards.

Spencer is a small town about half the size of Harmar, Ohio, situated on Spring Creek, a branch of the Kanawha, and can boast of a court-house of considerable dimensions and a number of handsome brick dwelling houses and stores. It has been in the possession of the home guards for some time back who were in the meantime besieged by about 700 secessionists. Evidence of this is sufficient to convince anyone of the fact, for the court house walls are literally peppered with bullet marks and

Lt. Col. William H. G. Adney

the blood still remains there of a home guard killed in the fight. Judge Peole, also a Union man, was killed in the fight. The secessionists were constrained to raise the siege last Friday after the Union men had made a sally and killed 20 or 25 of them.

Pvt. John Hechler, a member of Capt. Jewett Palmer's Company G, returned to "Camp Reedy," where another contemporary letter describes some of his experiences in the Roane and Wirt county areas:

Last Wednesday evening, a messenger came into Spencer from Camp Reedy on a jaded horse, with news that one of our baggage trains from Elizabeth had been surrounded and was in great danger of falling into the hands of the secessionists. Parts of the companies of Captains Palmer, Adney, Taylor and Devol were ordered to hold themselves in readiness to march at a moment's warning. At 3 a.m. we were called out and arrived here about 9 and found the train all right; nevertheless, it had been fired upon, and several of the horses wounded. One bayonet was

COLONEL HIRAM F. DEVOL

cut in two pieces by a ball from a Minie musket. The secessionists hereabouts are mostly armed with the ordinary huntsman's rifle.

Friday morning a detachment of men from several companies, under the command of Captain Palmer, started out to meet another train from Elizabeth under charge of Hill's cavalry which was a mile in advance was fired on the same spot where the train of Wednesday had been attacked, but before the infantry could come up the secessionists had fled to the woods. Fifty or sixty shots were exchanged and one of Hill's men was wounded in the thigh. None of the enemy was killed or wounded so far as is known. Nor can we encircle or take them, unless the major permits us to remain here until the snow flies, when we may possibly track them to their lair in the hills.

AFTER THEIR BRUSHES WITH DEATH AND BAPTISMS of fire in Roane county six companies of infantry set out on September 11, 1861, from Spencer. The infantry, which included Pvt. John Hechler, made a forced march to Summersville in Nicholas County, and one of the contemporary letters read: "We arrived at Summersville at 4 o'clock yesterday, after leaving 18 or 20 of our boys in the hospital at Sutton, the county seat of Braxton county, part with sore feet, and two or three with fever. Even this is better than expected considering the hard marching and sleeping which we did by the way. It was nothing uncommon for us to march 25 miles and then sleep on the bare ground with the stars shining brightly on us—when it did not rain.

A few days after John Hechler's arrival in Summersville his older brother George, still chafing from his enforced stay at home to harvest the crop and sow the wheat in September, signed his enlistment papers at Parkersburg.

4. The Young Volunteer

Camped in Parkersburg — Wrote War Letters
Sought Taverns — O. D. Was Minister

TWILIGHT WAS DESCENDING on Parkersburg on the evening of September 20, 1861. Heavy rains had fallen for several days, and Court Square was a sea of muck. Fortunately, the river banks had been lined with boulders making it easier to load and unload along the wharfs. But the Ohio River was at the highest ever known during September.

George Hechler stepped ashore at Parkersburg from the railroad steamer *Daniel Webster*, which had carried him across the river. He hoisted his clothing and equipment onto his back and started up 7th Street (at that time known as Pike Street). A shade under 5'8", young George was not an imposing figure as he plodded along with several buddies from Marietta, all bound to enlist in the Union Army for three-year hitches. He said very little as they moved through the streets of Parkersburg in the soft twilight. He was determined about one thing: to join up with Captain Jewett Palmer's Company. Jewett Palmer (later, four-time Mayor of Marietta) had those qualities of leadership which inspired confidence.

From the waterfront, George Hechler and his buddies went out the Staunton Pike until they reached a rich grove of oak trees. There, on one side of the Pike, was the imposing mansion built by William E. Stephenson in 1820. Across the pike in the grove was the 36th Ohio Volunteer Infantry, camped in tents. They had labeled their area as "Camp Union."

HERE AT CAMP UNION, George wrote the first of a long series of war letters to his sister Kate, who was in Marietta. The first letter did not say much, written as it was only a day after George had arrived in camp. It showed his general reticence. Later, when describing the details of battles, George was more graphic in his writing. His first letter, dated September 21, 1861, read as follows:

> Dear Sister:
>
> I will write to you soon. This time all I promise is to let you know how I get along soldiering. The same evening I started from Marietta I came into camp and enrolled my name, and well it was, for there were no more than 14 boys came down that evening to join Captain Palmer's company, which was just the number required to fill it, and so we have the only full company in the regiment. Our corporal told me yesterday that all the officers of our company had agreed not to touch liquor, and desired all of their men to do likewise, which I was glad to hear, so we have the prospect of having a temperate company.
>
> As to my own experiences of camp life I cannot say much as yet as I have only been here one day, but I think I shall like it first rate. I am yet well and hope you are. May hand is getting tired and I have the box you gave me for a table, and my blanket for a chair.
>
> Give my best respects to the inquiring folks up there—a good share for yourself, from your brother,
>
> George Hechler
> Address: Care of Captain Palmer, Parkersburg, Wood county, Virginia.

Fast-growing Parkersburg in 1861 was taking on the aspects of a "boom town." It was an important crossroads to the west. Visitors poured in to share the new-found wealth in the oil fields east of town. The Baltimore and Ohio Railroad disgorged new people every day, some to settle down in Parkersburg others to push on to find a homestead. With this shifting population, came the desire for that which irrigates parched throats, George Hechler saw its effects; hence his remark about the use of liquor in Company G, Jewett Palmer's company. But the market did not suffer when the troops pitched their tents at Camp Union.

THERE WAS A COOL, CLEAR SPRING of gurgling water a quarter of a mile from Camp Union. To many of the occupants of Camp Union, the spring did not prove to be sufficiently attractive for their parched throats. It remained for many of the soldiers to seek out the taverns in the town. (And the taverns were not handicapped by any prohibits or inhibitions against serving "liquor by the drink.")

The first regimental commander of the 36th was Lt. Col. Melvin Clarke, a Marietta lawyer, who was considerably annoyed by developments. The doughty colonel maintained his headquarters at the B & O Depot, a little distance from Camp Union. He was not amused when an inebriated enlisted man staggered in one evening and decided to sleep off the effects of a carousing night, and chose the roof of the depot. During the night he rolled off the roof and dropped about 20 feet into some "night soil" and was discovered snoring through filth the next morning.

Col. Clarke was firm and patient at first, urging local taverns not to serve his men while they were too obviously "high." Then he issued neighborly warnings to the establishments, which were doing a land-office business. The results could not be termed a sensational success.

EARLY IN OCTOBER, D-Day for a major operation arrived. Col. Clarke selected an evening when the officer of the day was Captain Warren Hollister of Company E, a former Methodist minister. The regimental commander detailed Capt. Hollister and 250 men to set forth and confiscated the liquor of those establishment which had defied his orders. Captain Hollister and his raiding party working steadily throughout Parkersburg until 11 p.m. and rounded up about $20,000 worth of liquors. One proprietor and his wife told Col. Clarke they were not in the least offended when Capt. Hollister carted off a vault with some $25,000 worth of additional fine wines, but the proprietor proposed to lock and seal his vault if he could get it back and then turn the key over to Col. Clarke as a good faith receipt. Col. Clarke readily went along with this sporting proposal.

Once this troublesome problem was cleared up, the boys at Camp y turned their attention to the perennial problem of how to keep dry. On the morning of Oct. 5, George Hechler was stirred from his blankets by 6 a.m. reveille. The ground was muddy and his blankets were sopping wet as he turned over. The rain had driven little rivulets underneath his tent. He pulled on his boots and outer clothing and staggered outside for reveille roll-call in Parkersburg's dawn light. All morning was spent "policing up" the soggy area. At lunch that day the men enjoyed baked beans, rice, bacon, hard bread and black coffee. After lunch, Pvt. Hechler had a little spare time to sit down and write the following letter to Sister Kate over in Marietta:

Dear Sister:

I again take the pen in my hand to write a few lines to you, as our stay in this camp after this will probably be short. We have no positive marching orders yet, but to judge from movements and preparations of the officers we shall leave today or tomorrow. I do not know where we will go, but I think Summersville is the place of our destination, by way of the river to Charleston, Va. I am yet quite well and like soldier-life (as much as I have seen of it) first-rate.

Your loving brother, George Hechler
Care of Captain Palmer,
Parkersburg, Wood County, Virginia

5. To Camp Piatt at Charleston, WV

Aboard the *Benjamin Franklin*
Man Overboard — Towering Mountains

In October of 1861 came the aftermath of torrential fall rains in Parkersburg—the flooding of the Ohio River. Down the Little Kanawha rushed hundreds of barrels of precious oil, oil tools and shanties, swept to destruction. The current was so fast at Parkersburg where the Little Kanawha flows into the Ohio that several men lost their lives trying to recover their possessions.

At noon of Saturday, Oct. 5, Pvt. George Hechler and his fellow soldiers of the 36th Ohio Volunteer Infantry Regiment received sudden orders at "Camp Union" in Parkersburg to strike tents. They marched through the Parkersburg streets to board the steamer *Benjamin Franklin* for the trip down the Ohio River.

The trip during the afternoon and early evening was like a picnic. Cheers resounded from people lining the river banks, and were answered by the throaty yells of the boys on board the *Benjamin Franklin*. Many flags were flying on both sides of the river as the steamboat made its way down past Blennerhassett Island and Belleville.

Passing Murraysville, the regiment spotted a huge crowd of the local citizenry who had fashioned a tremendous American flag which they proudly held up to view where it could be seen up and down the river. Major Corey the regimental band director had his men strike up a salute to the flag.

At Long Bottom, Racine and Ravenswood the girls predominated in the crowd, waving scarfs and kerchiefs. About sundown the *Benjamin Franklin* stopped at Pomeroy to take on coal. No sooner had the boat touched the wharf than many of the boys jumped ashore and started up the bank, and guards had to be sent out to round up the strays.

Pvt. Samuel B. Sample of Co. G did not feel just right about making the river trip. He had remarked to some of his messmates at Camp Union that morning that he did not expect to live more than a couple of days after he left Parkersburg. They all laughed at Pvt. Sample for advancing such a weird idea. Pvt. Sample told his messmates they might laugh at him if they chose but he stated firmly that his predictions usually came true.

IT WAS JUST AN HOUR BEFORE MIDNIGHT when the *Benjamin Franklin* stopped at Gallipolis to take a pilot aboard when Pvt. Hechler heard the cry of a man overboard. Pvt. Sample on passing by the cook house forward on the steamboat had stepped on a lump of coal which turned with him throwing him into the Ohio River. Several members of Company G manned a ferry skiff and rowed around the troop boat, and thence up and downstream several hundred yards, calling Sample's name, but all in vain. Several days later Sample's body was recovered. It was the first casualty since George Hechler had joined the company, and it was the first of a series of grim experiences he was to suffer.

Pvt. Hechler's account of the trip and his arrival at Camp Piatt, Charleston, are detailed in a letter he wrote to his sister Kate in Marietta dated October 10, 1861:

> October 10, 1861
> Dear Sister:
>
> You know before this of our departure from Parkersburg. The same evening about sundown we stopped at Pomeroy to take on coal: about eleven we stopped at Gallipolis to take a pilot aboard, when suddenly the cry of a man overboard was heard, connected with the name of one of the boys of our Company. He could not be found again. I laid myself down on the deck of

the boat but could not sleep much. About four the next morning the boat was lying near the shore and I was told we were 24 miles up the Kanawha River. At daylight the boat was again pushed out and we ascended the rather dreary looking stream. We soon could see that we now were in a slave country by the large farm houses, with small ones around them and darkeys in front cheering like fine fellows.

Soon the hills presented themselves to our view. And then Charleston was in sight, and the breastwork which ex-Governor Wise had thrown up partly up the hill to prevent the navigation of the river by the Federal troops on boats. All along we were received with cheers, waving of the stars and stripes on the bank being not uncommon.

At Charleston we saw the effects of the late freshet. One house standing near the river had lost one entire wall from being undermined by the water. The buildings of Charleston are mostly of brick and have a fine appearance from the river. The banks were lined with soldiers and soon a camp made its appearance above the town. We now were told we should go up the river as far as the boat would go. After going about 12 miles further the boat landed and after about one hour's delay we were ordered to go on shore. We found our camp was to be a field of wheat stubbles, being rather soft under-foot from the continual rain.

The 34th Ohio Guards are encamped in an adjoining field. Day before yesterday about 25 of them went out and came back in the evening with 110 head of cattle, the most of them being marked "J. D." (Jefferson Davis) and consequently considered contraband. We now have fresh beef for several meals. It eats good.

There are some rather steep hills here on each side of the bottom. On the top of the hill behind our camp is a rock, the front of which is higher that the top of the trees standing before it. The hill is nearly a mile high and soldiers in camp look about two feet high from the top of the rock. I found some chestnuts on this hill and we have some paw paws, apples and pumpkins now. Above Charleston are the celebrated salt works, some of which are burned, the ruins of which represent the folly of secession.

Week before last the Guards had an engagement which

killed their Colonel and routed them completely, they losing four killed and five wounded. Our Second Lieutenant came down day before yesterday. He says the boys are at Summersville and are all in good health.

I am yet well, and hope you are, from

Your brother,
GEORGE

P.S. Write soon and send your letter to Camp Piatt, Kanawha County, Virginia.

PVT. GEORGE HECHLER looked around him at Camp Piatt, he marveled at the landscape of the Kanawha Valley. The hills of home near Marietta seemed like little man-made mounds in contrast to the towering mountains on either side of the Kanawha River. (The site of Camp Piatt is in 2011 occupied by the huge DuPont plant at Belle.) The mountains washed down great amounts of mud and water into the camping areas. So George was glad at last when the signal was given to strike tents and make ready for the 60-mile march to join the rest of Company G of the 36th Regiment, including his Brother John, at Summersville.

6. Autumn of 1861

60-mile March — Went For Straw — Paraded Into Camp

THE OHIO RIVER was running high in October, 1861. Troop steamers had little trouble with sand bars and low water, as they did in the summertime. When Pvt. George Hechler and his buddies left Parkersburg in October, they were hoping the war would be over by the turn of the year. Ten months later they returned to Parkersburg, sadder and wiser, their ranks thinned by battle and disease.

When the leaves were falling in 1861, George felt that the fortunes of the Confederacy were also fluttering to the ground. It took the shock of cold steel in battle to revise Hechler's estimate of the situation.

After their boat trip down the Ohio and up the Kanawha to Charleston and a few days at Camp Piatt (at Belle, West Virginia), Hechler's company started its 60-mile march to Summersville in Nicholas county. Forty wagon trains rumbled through the mud toward Summersville, slowing the march and making it hard to stay in ranks. An enterprising Negro along the way peddled hard cider for a quarter a pint cup-full and charged a dollar to fill a two-quart canteen. Business was brisk. The unusually large knot of soldiers did not take long to attract the attention of a fussing and fuming Major, who finally located the source of all this liquid joy.

"This will stop, right this minute," barked the Major with finality.

The Negro slave, jingling coins in his jeans, bared his white dentures and smiled: "I doan care. I'se get de money for all I solded."

For a moment the Major softened and asked: "And how much did you solded?"

"Ah reckons about two barrels," drawled the entrepreneur.

The men fell back into ranks and pressed forward in the mud and rain, until after dark. Then they pitched tents in a soft, cutover stubblefield. Before the camp fires started to burn to dry out the men, a mud-caked private appeared at Hechler's tent with a load of fresh straw.

"PLENTY OF GOOD STRAW in a stack across the road," the splattered one told Hechler, who lost no time in starting after it. Across the road he fell into a big, blind mud-hole, three or four feet deep. Raucous laughter and cries of "There goes another one," greeted him. There were plenty of men who went for straw that night, and the straw was really there, but nearly everybody had the initiation of falling into the mud-hole to the delight of many who had also gotten their mud-baths. It was their first really good belly-laugh since joining the army, and it was amazing how it brought the men closer together.

The Sabbath fell on October 20. Reveille was at 5:30 A.M., the men breakfasted at 6, and were on the march at 7 a.m. Along the road the men and women waved their hats and sunbonnets. This was the area from which the Confederate General (and former Governor of Virginia) Henry A. Wise had retreated. As Pvt. Hechler and members of his company passed along they observed an elderly colored lady jumping up and down, with tears running down her check, shouting: "Hurrah for der Union!" One of the Hechler's platoon yelled: "Can we whip Massa Wise?" The elderly lady grinned: "Y'all can't ketch Massa Wise. He done run too fast!"

On the men pressed to Kanawha Falls, where they paused for a few hours to rest and admire one of nature's rare creations which brings pride to every West Virginian. There the tired and muddy boys in blue peeled off their splattered clothes and despite the cool nip in the air they took showers by standing on a solid rock platform. In the rapid, rushing, rock, boisterous New River, Company G of the 36th Ohio Volunteer Infantry had their first thorough clean-up since leaving Parkersburg.

Lt. Col. Melvin Clarke

For the next few days they inched closer to Summersville and George Hechler's reunion with his brother John who had already arrived at the Summersville camp. At the foot of Big Elk Mountain there was a halt for rest and supper o'pork, raw salt and crackers. Then the rough ascent of the mountain followed complete with rocks, quagmires of mud, roots, fallen trees, handsful of dirt, slipping and skidding. About 15 miles from Summersville, the regimental commander, Col. Clarke of Marietta, drew up the column to a halt and went up and down the line asking if they should push on to Summersville despite the fact it was after dark. It was raining hard, and the men were tired, miserable and wet to the skin. But suddenly a cheery voice from the darkness sang out, loud and clear: "Just as you say, Colonel. If they are needing us bad up there at Summersville, we ought to be there to protect them!"

Roars of laughter swept the ranks. Col. Clarke said: "Well, it's not as bad as all that, and the wagonmaster tells me our horses can't pull another yard, so here we'll stop for the night."

THE NEXT MORNING at 7:30, after a breakfast of crackers and sow-belly, they were on their way, reaching Summersville with flags flying and bands playing, at about two o'clock in the afternoon. The troops at Summersville, including Brother John were lined up and cheered lustily as the tired marchers straightened up and paraded into camp.

It took a few days before George Hechler could settle down, and then he wrote the following letter to his sister Kate in Marietta:

Dear Sister:

I received your letter last night and was glad to hear from you.

We arrived here one week ago, Tuesday afternoon. Wednesday night, about 10 o'clock, the sergeant commenced calling the roll (most of us were in a sound slumber), but leaving out a good many names. As we got into ranks, we anticipated a scout, and sound found it to be the object as our horse sacks were filled with provisions. The next forenoon we came to a house where the Captain seemed to want to look at, but the man there saw us come and had run away. We went skulking about the woods nearly all night, with no success other than to catch two Secesh. We returned to the house of Mr. Smith again (that was the gentleman's name), dividing into three squads. We approached the house and heard several guns fired. Mr. Smith had seventeen beehives, on which we went to work and soon everyone, the Captain not excepted, had his hands full of honey trickling down his face and hands.

The next night some of them gathered near the house, but did not come near enough for our rifles. We had a good breakfast the next morning of fresh beef and honey. Part of the company was now sent toward home with Smith's cattle, while the rest went scouting over the hill without success—only a little more honey.

We have fared tolerably well so far, but there are fears of our running out of bread. I have three and John has two pairs of socks—enough at present. I do not think we can wear mittens because we want to use each finger separately. A comforter might come in handy sometimes. I got a good overcoat yesterday with a high collar to it, and as my neck is short it nearly covers my ears.

I do not want to pack any more than the absolutely necessary clothing, so I will let you know when to send any of the things.

Brother John wrote several letters before he came to Summersville, and started two since I came here. We are both well at the present time.

We are having more cool weather. The ground was frozen this morning, and the meadows have a white frost which looks like a light snow. The leaves are nearly all off the trees and Fair Dame Nature is beginning to rest, to awake, as we hope, next Spring in new life. But this country will not look as pleasant, I fear, as it has before, for it is nearly destitute of inhabitants around the village of Summersville.

I remember well our loving Mother. Though young then, I have her image ever before my mind. How calm and lovely she looked upon us. But we ought not to lament her loss as we can get to see her in a better world if we try.

Your affectionate brother, George

7. Commanding the 36th

Military Training — Address at Marietta College
Indian Fighter

After his trip down the Ohio River by steamboat from Parkersburg, and his 60-mile march from Charleston to Summersville, Pvt. George Hechler rejoined his brother John who had already arrived in Summersville. The two young brothers reviewed their experiences since leaving their home on Harmar Hill, Marietta, to join the Union army.

One of the first orders of business in Hechler's regiment was organization and training for the severe and bloody conflicts ahead. At the time of his enlistment in Parkersburg on September 20, 1861, Pvt. George Hechler found that his company included mainly young men from the Marietta and Washington county areas. Many of his buddies were physically fit, eager and energetic youngsters who lacked only one thing—Army training.

This is why it was so important that the 36th Ohio Volunteer Infantry Regiment secure capable officers with the military experience to conduct thorough training. The first two officers of Hechler's regiment were leading citizens of Marietta—Lt. Col. Melvin Clarke and Major E. B. Andrews.

Melvin Clarke was one of the leading lawyers of Marietta, but before studying law he taught school for several years as an assistant to the Rev. Hawks in Parkersburg. He also taught in Newport, Washington county. After the sweeping Confederate victory at the first battle of Bull Run. Melvin Clarke received a telegram from

Brig. Gen. George Crook

Gen. Philip Henry Sheridan

Congressman William P. Cutler asking Clarke to raise an infantry regiment. Commissioned on July 30, 1861, Lt. Col. Clarke fought bravely in the early engagements of the 36th, until he fell mortally wounded at the battle of Antietam. Col. Clarke's widow, Sophia Browning, survived him and lived for many years with their three children at Belpre.

Ebenezer B. Andrews, minister of the gospel and teacher, came to Marietta in 1851 to deliver an address to the Marietta College alumni at commencement time. He made such an impression as an orator and a man of culture that he was asked to be a member of the faculty at Marietta College in the field of natural sciences. Professor Beach one of Professor Andrews' pupils wrote:

> In his college work, Professor Andrews early became especially interested in geological investigations and during his stay here the study of geology was made very prominent. His teaching in this department was suggestive and stimulating. His students

> were sure to think geology a great and living science. During a series of years, he conducted his senior classes on exploring expeditions which will not be forgotten by any who participated in them. The writer remembers with much interest the explorations made by the Class of 1859 through the wildest parts of Washington county, and which occupied five days. The enthusiasm of the professor, as well as his unfailing good humor and his rich resources of wit and anecdote, made it a memorable journey to the young men who followed him.

ACTUALLY, PROFESSOR ANDREWS proved to be a better geologist than a military man. Commissioned as a major in Hechler's regiment, he later became regimental commander for a brief period but for various reasons and by mutual consent he resigned his commission and returned to teach at Marietta College in 1863. Later, he was made assistant geologist of the Ohio Geological Survey. Professor Andrews died at Lancaster, Ohio in 1880.

One of Professor Andrews' greatest contributions to Hechler's regiment was to insist that the fullest possible effort be made to secure the services of professionally trained military man at an early date.

The man secured for the position of commanding officer of the 36th Regiment was to Pvt. Hechler one of the Civil War's real heroes: General George Crook, who before and after the Civil War gained a wide reputation as an Indian fighter.

George Crook had been Phil Sheridan's room-mate in the West Point Class of 1852. Crook was a man of medium size, with light hair and sandy beard, with a diffident and rather shy manner. His whole style was quiet and reticent. His voice was so light and he was so laconic in speech that this, with his other characteristics, caused it to be commonly said of General Crook that he had been so long fighting Indians on the frontier that he had acquired some of their traits and habits. His system of discipline was based on these peculiarities. Crook aimed at a stoical command of himself as a means of commanding others, and avoided a noisy bluster of every sort. Pvt. Hechler and his buddies soon learned to have the greatest confidence in him as a leader and a military officer.

After the Battle of Bull Run, Crook, then a captain in the Regular Army, called on his Congressman, Ohio Representative Robert C. Schenck (a former professor at Miami University), who had first appointed Schenck to West Point, Schenck confronted President Lincoln and asked him to have Crook transferred to command a volunteer infantry regiment. According to Crook:

> Mr. Lincoln said no, that he never interfered with the running of any branches of the government any more than he would try to mend a watch, for, should he put his foot in it, it would never run again. Crook added this comment about the Great Emancipator: "This gave me a good opportunity to examine President Lincoln's personal appearance. He was the most ungainly man I had ever seen, particularly his legs and feet."

Shortly thereafter, Governor Dennison of Ohio appointed George Crook as a full colonel to command the 36th Ohio Volunteer Infantry Regiment. Pvts. George and John Hechler were delighted when the new commander arrived at their camp in Summersville. The Marietta Intelligencer reported on October 9, 1861: "Colonel, Crook has taken the hearts of the soldiers by storm. He is very popular and is looked upon as an officer of superior ability."

8. The Winter of 1861

Camp Fever — Taken To Hospital On His Feet Again

THE WINTRY WINDS of December whistled through the Union camp, across the rolling hills and plains of Nicholas county. Pvts. George and John Hechler threw themselves energetically into the task of sawing up the tall timber girdling the camp, carting it to an assembly point, and helping to build a tremendous drill house for the regiment.

Such a hammering and chopping and chattering arose as had never before been heard in the vicinity! Regimental commander Col. George Crook, Indian fighter and West Point disciplinarian was determined that his raw and green troops should be drilled and trained until they would act mechanically but fearlessly in battle. Thus, the drill shed, nearly 1,000 feet in length, which made it possible for the determined colonel to drill his men in fair weather or foul.

Every day, in snow, sleet or rain, the men went out to drill. Some fell by the wayside. The dreaded "camp fever" struck a terrible blow in Hechler's regiment. At one time over 300 men in the regiment were on the sick list. Early in December, the regiment sadly assembled for the funeral of Pvt. Joe Corpp. To happy-go-lucky John Hechler, with the strength of an ox and the light heart of a perpetually happy person, the funeral had little effect. But to George Hechler, a serious and purposeful oldest son, the burial of Joe Corpp shook him deeply. Joe was the fifth man in Company G to die since the company had left Parkersburg two months before.

"FIVE DEATHS," thought George to himself. "How long can we go on this way with disease and death stalking the camp, killing the flower of our men before the Rebels have fired a shot?" George's knees weakened and sagged. That evening they took him to the hospital.

On December 28, 1861, George had enough strength to write the following letter to his sister Kate in Marietta:

> My dear Sister:
>
> I received your letter of the 10th a few days ago, and was very glad to hear from you. I could not answer your letter any sooner as I had the camp fever, but I am now nearly well again. Most of the boys, I believe, will have to have more or less of it. I have been able to be up all the time but about two hours when I had to lay down to sleep. I think we have good surgeons in our regiment, but in spite of their efforts some have died. There are about 40 or more in the hospital, most of them getting better.
>
> John is well and wrote a letter yesterday full of rumors. We have been paid up to the first of November, and there is talk that we will be paid in a few days up to the first of next month. I shall send my money the first chance I get.
>
> We have still nice times here, and plenty to eat and I like a soldier's life. I think I shall be able for duty in a few days. My bed feels rather hard since I am getting better.
>
> I have not received any letter from Father since the 6th of this month. Does anyone come to you often, and who comes? We have had fine weather nearly all this month, but the nights are very cold.
>
> Excuse poor writing, as my hand is yet a little nervous. I must close this letter.
>
> I remain, your loving brother, George

ON NEW YEAR'S DAY, 1862, George was on his feet again, and he wrote his sister Kate with a bold, firm hand:

My Dear Sister:

I take my pen in hand to inform you that we are well at present and I hope these few lines will find you well. John received his letter dated the 22nd a few days ago, and I received the papers the same day. He wrote an answer last night.

We make our red ink out of the juice of polk berries, a little brown sugar and rain water.

I thought your letter was short, but long enough to tell me the most of the news. We had rather a dry Christmas but we are merry every day. Last night about 7:00 o'clock we received the stirring orders to cook two days rations now. We commenced speculating as to the whereabouts of our going, but this is yet a mystery to us here. I did not go because I did not think I was strong enough to stand it yet.

About 11:00 o'clock last night we were roused again to receive our pay up to the first of January. Enclosed I send 80 dollars, 5 of which John wishes you to keep for yourself and give the rest to Father. Tell him 35 is from me and the other from John. Tell him I did think of keeping my money, but as he pays high interest rates I will let him have all I can spare.

John wants to know if you received a letter with a gold dollar in it. I shall send this letter by Mr. Barber (the Quartermaster) but I do not know yet when he is going. He may not go out for over a week yet, as I think all of our field officers went out this morning and he will probably stay till they return.

I wish you a Happy New Year. This is New Year's Day and it will long be passed before this can reach you.

Well, I had a good piece of pie and good light bread and turkey meat for breakfast. We have to buy such things, but they make good meals for a little change.

Do not trouble yourself about seeing us now, but the general belief here is that we shall all see our friends about next June if we live.

I remain, your loving brother, GEORGE HECHLER

A few days later, Brother John penned the following letter to Sister Kate in Marietta:

Summersville, Va
The 6th of January, 1862

My Dear Sister:

It is with pleasure that I set myself down to inform you that I am well and hearty and George is able for duty now.

The weather is cold and snow on the ground is about four inches deep. We have to drill every day as we have built a house to drill in, it is one thousand feet long. You ask me in your letter how it came that our company was not filled up. It was full some time ago but it is not now, there are six of our company died with the fever, and two of our company deserted.

We have been paid for all our time and I suppose that you will know it before these few lines reach you. Have sent you a letter with a gold dollar in it. I wish you would let me send more. In your last letter you told me that you had sent a letter some time before you wrote George the letter, but I have not received it yet.

I suppose you know all the news before this time, as George has been writing some letters since we came back. I was in it, and George has told you all about it.

I wish you would send some stamps, about 25 of them, as we cannot get them here, and I will want to send some letters to some places where I would like to pay respects.

I like soldiering better than any other work. Will you send me some socks, if this letter reaches you, as they are better than some are. We have plenty of uniforms for some time and are armed well.

Give my best respects to the old folks and all my friends.

I remain, your affectionate brother, JOHN

9. Scouting in the Mountains

Skirmish in West Virginia
Killed With Empty Rifle — "Deer Lick" in Camp

THE FIRST MAJOR CLASH of arms in which Pvt. Hechler took part was at Lewisburg in May of 1862, following which he was wounded in the bloody battle of Antietam in September. In the early months of 1862, he spent in thorough training with his regiment—a schedule which produced brilliant results on the battlefield when the regiment was thrown into action.

In the early days of January, George was still recovering from a serious bout of the camp fever which had killed five members of his own company. Brother John, as the following letter indicated, played a big part in one of the "scouts" or minor skirmishes which took place in January, George wrote on January 6, 1862 to his sister Kate in Marietta:

Dear Sister:

I regret I was not stout enough to go out on the scout, but it may have been for my best. All of the able men of six companies started for Sutton, a distance of about 35 miles, Sutton had been burned a day or two before by the Rebels and companies of cavalry stationed there were scared away. Though they fought from noon 'til dark, it seems they kept well out of the range of each other's guns as there was not a man killed on either side.

After 15 miles' travel, a messenger met them, stating that the bridge across the Elk River was burned and the Rebels had left there. Colonel Crook, Lt. Col. Clarke, two companies, and some that had sore feet, turned back. Nearly 200 started for a three day scout in the mountains.

The first day they only saw a squad. But on the second day they were suddenly fired on from three sides of the hill. Brother John was behind the company, coming out of a large storehouse (empty) which they had set on fire. The balls rained around him without one touching. He made for the nearest bushes. Around there more than a thousand acres are more like weeds than woods. Soon John saw three men standing in one group, nearly in range, hurrahing for Jeff Davis. His rifle was loaded, contrary to the rules, with two balls. He fired, and all fell. One, however, crawled away on his hands and feet.

Another of our men ran after one, catching him, but the Rebel struck at him with his rifle. However, his luck was off and he fell, struck by the butt of a rifle. The Rebel was armed with one rifle, & one revolver and a big Bowie knife. Our man was a member of Company D. He set his foot on the neck of the Rebel, took his revolver, and killed him with his own weapon.

The woods and hills seemed to be hurrahing for Jeff Davis, but as soon as our men came on top of the hills all cheering was changed into groans of the wounded and curses of the dying. Our men soon saw some of the F.F.V. ("Fast-Flying Virginians") and they acknowledged that there was no use for them to try and catch them. All fighting was over in less than one hour. We lost only three in wounded two slightly and one through the lung, but he is getting better. He was able to ride home horseback. The surgeon says that no body of men could have shown less fear than our men did.

Your affectionate brother, GEORGE

OTHER MEMBERS of George's company reported that the remarkable part of the story George wrote was that the Rebel soldier referred to was actually killed by a man with an empty rifle.

Several inches of snow blanketed the ground in the early days of January. The hills and valleys were covered, making it difficult to obscure the traces of the Rebel "bushwhackers" when they ventured close to camp. Several pigs were running around the post, which caused considerable annoyance at first, but soon from some mysterious source succulent, tender, fresh pork began to appear on the menu at mess time.

At the quartermaster depot in camp, several barrels of salt were stashed away. One of them burst open, and from then on the tracks of deer were observed in the snow. They had formed a "deer lick" at the camp.

On January 11, 1862, George Hechler wrote a brief note to his sister:

> My Dear Sister:
>
> I received your letter of the 2nd of January a few days ago. Was glad to hear from you.
>
> I have gotten well again, but am at times subject to severe attacks of nervous headache. I think in a short time I shall get rid of it if I don't read too much, as my eyes appear weak yet.
>
> This morning the wagons started out, for corn I guess. We have no news here. Rumors are as plenty as pies and apples, and the latter articles have been plenty in camp for the last two weeks, but of poor quality. The crust of some of the pies might be used for sole leather.
>
> Your ever loving brother, GEORGE

The huckster with the leather pies and the green apples were the inevitable part of camp life, and were the butt of many jokes. One day a prankster cut a hole in the huckster's bag of apples, and while he scurried around to retrieve the bobbing apples, a couple of the boys boldly lifted the unguarded pies. It was just one way of expressing unanimous distaste for the high-priced insults to the collective stomachs of the men.

As January wore on, even more intensive drills were held. Five to seven hours a day, wet or dry, Colonel Crook had his regiment march down the slag walks, covered with sawdust and ground tanbark to the covered, 800 foot drill shed.

George Hechler contemplated that perhaps one reason Colonel Crook was drilling his men so vigorously was to keep their minds off their relatives and friends, and home and hearth. He also discovered, however, that the constant drilling was slowly molding the regiment into an effective fighting unit. As one member of the company put it: "It hardly seems that such a great change could be wrought in so short a time. It not only makes us understand, but it assures confidence within ourselves, and to a great degree helps us get to know each other, relying upon and in turn being relied upon."

10. Optimism Turns to Restlessness

In the early months of the Civil War, after the shock of the defeat in the first Battle of Bull Run had worn off, the Union forces were gripped with a wave of excessive optimism. Pvt. George Hechler got caught up with this spirit, and wrote to his sister in Marietta on February 6, 1862, indicating his belief that the war would be over soon:

> My Dear Sister:
>
> We have received good news up here. It seems favorable to our cause and if our country moves onward the war must soon come to a close. But how can it be carried on long at the rate it is now? The supplies of the Rebels must be nearly exhausted, to judge from prices, as a Negro recently stated them to us. He is rather reserved in speaking freely but I think this Negro speaks the truth. He says corn is a dollar per bushel in the South; wheat one and one half to two dollars; rice twenty cents a pound; coffee, one dollar; salt, from ten to twelve or twelve and one-half cents a pound and then it is almost impossible to get any. He has been a slave who was down in South Carolina with his master last summer. They had nothing to eat there then but rice and sweet potatoes, with a little beef. He said sugar and coffee was then a luxury. What is it now?
>
> We would love to share in the victories of the southwest, but are now more than satisfied to remain where we are till our officers see fit or order us into combat. The weather has now set in cold and

we have had deep snow for several days. Lewisburg, it is thought by some, will be our next place of operation in this quarter.

Your affectionate brother GEORGE

Six days later, On February 12, Pvt. Hechler penned another letter to his sister in Marietta expressing his personal opinions of Albert Gallatin Jenkins, one of the great Confederate cavalry officers who also served two terms in the House of Representatives from the Ohio Valley area. (Jenkins made his home in Greenbottom, Cabell County, two miles south of the Mason County line and made a famous raid into Ravenswood, crossing the river into Ohio. In November, 1861, he had routed the Union forces in Guyandotte in a bloody battle which steeled the Union men to express the kind of opinion Pvt. Hechler does in the following letter.) At that time a colonel, Jenkins was later promoted to Brigadier General, and was killed in 1864 in the battle of Cloyd's Mountain. Here is Pvt. Hechler's February 12 letter to sister Kate in Marietta:

Dear Sister:

Rumors are circulating in camp that Colonel Jenkins the same who murdered our men at Guyandotte, is gathering 1,600 men, all cavalry, to pay us a visit soon. Well, let him come, we will give him and his whole band of thieves a warm reception. This, however, is contradicted by some Negroes who escaped from their masters and came into camp yesterday. They all have employment in camp.

The five Negroes are all fine, intelligent looking men. They say the Rebel force in Lewisburg is about 15 or 16 hundred, of which nearly two-thirds is militia. I do not think we will have much fighting to do unless we are soon moved from here, of which there is little prospect now. This place appears now nearly like home, since we have been here so long. We drill every day, and if the regiment improves in the next six weeks as it has in the past six, the 36th Regiment need not be ashamed to show itself in combat.

Yesterday, we received the news about the victories our men won, one of them nearly a complete success, Kate, I think May or June will again find our country at peace and if the Lord spares me I think we will soon have the pleasure of meeting and have a talk about good old times. But this cannot be any sooner than the end of the war.

I remain, your loving brother, GEORGE

On February 26, Pvt. Hechler wrote that his regiment was still drilling in the staging area:

My Dear Sister:

We are well at present (all but a little cold.) We have had very bad weather here lately, it changes about twice a day and the roads are almost impassable. Although we are still here, we had orders the other day to pack all the clothes we could not carry and send them home. Our tents came in day before yesterday with a stove to each tent, so we may be ordered away from here any day.

Edward Doudle and I put some clothes into a box to send to Marietta. I think we shall send it tomorrow. I have a shirt, comforter, and a pair of shoes, and the mittens you sent to me. I have got a pair of gloves now that I bought for 25 cents. There were sent to Lieutenant Nye from home, but were too large for him. Some of the things I am sending home are rather dirty, but excuse my laziness. You can do with the things what you please.

Our Mess has just hired a darkey for a cook. He came in this evening from near Lewisburg. He started from his master Sunday morning. There are seven in camp now that have come in lately. They are well pleased with their new conditions.

Your affectionate brother, GEORGE

In mid-March, despite some brushes and skirmishes with the Rebel bushwhackers, Pvt. Hechler was getting a little restless at the

LT. REUBEN L. NYE

"over-trained inactivity" of his combat regiment. President Lincoln too, was getting restless with General George McClellan. Here is how Pvt. Hechler describes the situation in a letter to his sister on March 15, 1862

My Dear Sister:

Last week two companies of our regiment started out, the one to Sutton and the other out into the country. The one from Sutton brought back six prisoners but the other did not do anything.

Monday forenoon it was rumored in camp that some Rebel cavalry had been seen about four miles from here across Gauley River, and Companies F and G started in different directions. Our company went to the river. When we stopped, Captain Palmer called on 20 men to cross the river with him. On the other side we left eight scattered along for sentinels in hearing distance, and the rest went out the road about five miles but could not find any enemy. I was with them. That was the last of the secesh cavalry rumor for the time being. Company F came back the next day having some tired legs and sore feet.

Yesterday evening a telegraphic dispatcher came in announcing that General Fremont was appointed commander of this department. This is not yet confirmed, but there were some cheers heard for Fremont. We are getting really tired of laying still, and it is generally believed Fremont would be the man for us. We may have to move soon now, as the sick that are not likely to get well soon were sent to the General hospital today.

Brother John and I are both well and getting along fine,

Your affectionate brother, GEORGE

11. The Fierce Pride of the 36th Regiment

Ohio Regiment — Well-Trained Clear Countryside Yearned For Action

ONE OF THE BEST CLUES to Pvt. Hechler's regiment was contained in an elaborate ad carried in the January 18, 1862 edition of The Marietta Home News. The ad read:

RECRUITS WANTED FOR THE
36th Regiment. Ohio Volunteers

> If there are any good men in this county which wish to enlist, now is the time to join one of the best regiments in the service. The whole regiment is armed with Enfield rifles, and well-equipped in every respect, and has one of the best commanders in the service. The regiment is well-organized and Col. George Crook is a military man all over, possessing all of the good qualities of a military man, without tyranny and red tape-ism that belong to most West Point men. While he is firm and has as much decision as any man ought to have, yet he is agreeable and pleasant to his officers and men. Everything moves in the regiment in perfect order and in military style. The worst wish I ever heard against Colonel Crook was that he had a wife and six children, thinking that he could then sympathize with those that are in that situation, and would not be so reluctant in granting leaves of absence.

The ad in the Marietta newspaper revealed the intense pride the men held for their regiment and its commander. Col. Crook. (The last sentence of the ad refers to the fact that the commander of the 36th regiment did not marry until after the war was over, and this may have made him a rougher taskmaster with not quite as much sympathy for family problems of his men.)

PRIOR TO THE BIG BATTLE of Lewisburg in May of 1862—the first clash of arms in which Pvt. Hechler engaged—the regiment continued its intensive training and scouts and skirmishes to clean the countryside of bushwhackers. On March 25, 1862, Pvt. Hechler wrote to his sister Kate in Marietta:

> Dear Sister:
>
> I take this beautiful evening to write a few lines to you.
>
> Well, we have had very bad weather now for about a week, till this evening. I want to tell you a little about the scout we had last week. It did not pay very big, but we had a big time of it. Last Tuesday, just one week ago today, a bushwhacker came in to take the Oath of Allegiance to the Government, stating that the Rebels were drafting and pressing every man into their service who could bear arms, between the ages of 15 and 50, and that they were not willing to fight for them.
>
> Some of them were familiar with the spot where the cavalry had annoyed us a great deal, and offered to guide us to the spot where they were camped. They said there were about 40 or 50 of them, all told. So Wednesday we started about 60 strong, half of the number from our Company G, and the other half from Company D. The place is about 35 miles from Summersville, and it was intended that the Rebels be surprised on Friday morning about daylight.
>
> Wednesday afternoon it rained and we stopped at a barn. The next day before noon, a man came in who said he had come to give himself up, and his story was believed. Soon it commenced

raining again and at about seven in the evening we halted a few miles from our destination, anxiously waiting for midnight. Now the rain commenced pouring down, and froze as it fell, the snow already being about two inches deep. We could hardly start a fire, and after we did get one started it was all smoke. We had to stir about to keep warm, and the rain soon turned to snow. But we were all in good spirits because our plan so far had succeeded and this time we were not yet discovered by the Rebels. It seemed likely our trip was going to pay, but about ten o'clock we discovered that the prisoner had gone, since he had not been guarded and could not anywhere be found.

The conclusion now was that he had gone to tell the Rebels of our coming, so guards were put out for now we were in danger of being taken by surprise in turn. Before dawn our company commanders, Captains Palmer and Dunham, decided on turning back without going any farther forward. The Rebels could by daylight go to Lewisburg and bring a force of about 400 against us from there, it being only a short distance away, and knowing our number the contest would have been too unequal.

So a little before daybreak we started toward Summersville with our horse sacks about empty, and a distance of 32 miles to travel by the mountain route. This is nothing but a foot-path cut through the woods in nearly a straight course, disregarding mountain or creek. In the first 18 miles there is only one house, the rest of the way about 8 or 10. The snow was about six inches deep and commenced melting after the sun rose, but the sky soon clouded up and again it rained. Saturday evening we came back to town with plenty of sore feet and hungry stomachs.

We got a little cornbread and meat along the road. The meat had never been salted, but dried fresh, so it did not taste very good to us. We now learn that 36 of the militia had come in the next day after we started, all armed after the fashion of Southern celebrated soldiers, some having muskets, some rifles, others shot-guns, others only axes. In all about 75 came in last week, but are all gone again from here now. Today, a train of provisions arrived here, and some will be in tomorrow, so we will have enough here for the month of April. This don't look like moving!

I am quite well and so is Brother John, but must close now as it is time for roll-call, perhaps before I get this folded.

I remain, your affectionate brother, George

P.S. The drum commenced beating as I was writing my name but I have about ten more minutes until Taps to put this up in.

AS MARCH DREW TO A CLOSE, the men in the 36th Regiment yearned for action. They were a few notches above the bounty-jumpers and miscellaneous draftees who composed some units of the Union Army, and they had a fierce pride in the condition of their unit and its command. The regimental commander Col. George Crook, was in later years acknowledged by General Sherman to be "the greatest Indian fighter and manager the United States Army every had." Crook did not rank high scholastically at West Point, but he was a genius at training and leading his men. Col. Crook later wrote in his autobiography of some of his problems with Pvt. Hechler's regiment:

> They were mostly from the country, and had been taken from their plows with such clothing as they happened to have on. They were as rare as a piece of beef-steak. Officers as well as men knew nothing of what was expected of them. They thought all they had to do was fight, and though that drill and discipline was entirely unnecessary, thought it only a waste of time, and that they could fight just as well as they were, etc. I had repeated talks with the officers, and we would have a mutual understanding, I explained I would not expect too much of them, but on their part they must learn their profession, and those who failed would have to give way to others who would, and that they were not the judges as to whether or not a knowledge of their profession was necessary. I must say that I never saw a more willing set of men in my life.

"Never in all my life did I work so hard, mentally and physically, as I did through this winter." Col. Crook wrote later in his autobiography.

And Pvt. Hechler and the men of his regiment hardened into a well–disciplined fighting machine under Crook's patient leadership. With this kind of training, they were ready for action when the bugles sounded and when the cannon thundered among the laurel.

12. The Miseries of Camp Life

Fatalism — Food is Challenge
Routine Changes — Alive and Well

THERE IS A KIND OF FATALISM about the common soldier in war. The excitement of combat, coupled with a desire not to let one's buddies down, makes a soldier forget the terror of bullets. But keep a soldier cooped up without action, and he will gripe and swear and get the miseries.

"We are getting really tired of this place and the lonesomeness of camp life," wrote Pvt. Hechler to his sister on March 30, 1862. "All are wishing for forward movement since the weather commenced getting warm and the good news comes in from every quarter."

Pvt. Hechler had another gripe against the Army. They fined him for losing a minor piece of his equipment. This was unusual for such a thorough and careful man that he was, and he felt somebody had performed a "moonlight requisition" by carefully lifting the equipment. "We were paid off yesterday up to the first of March," wrote Pvt. Hechler, "but I did not get much money as I had drawn considerable more clothing than was allowed me for the time I have been in service. Uncle Sam would have us all settle up our accounts with him, but he better look sharp or the next time we settle up we will empty his pockets for him, because the most of us have nearly clothes enough for the next six months."

Still and all, Pvt. Hechler was not as bad off as another member of the regiment upon whom the following court–martial sentence was imposed: "In that said Private John Danner did on the 13th

General William Rosecrans

day of April, 1862, sell one pair of drawers which he had previously drawn from the United States Army, the Court do therefore sentence him, Private John Danner, to forfeit from his pay an amount equal to the price of the pair of drawers."

Getting enough of the right kind of food was also a challenge in camp. Some of the soldiers noticed that the cakes served in camp, termed "dodgers" by some men, would more aptly be termed "cannon balls." Pvt. Hechler and his fellow members of Company G noted that there is a painful rumor afloat in camp that General Rosecrans is about to issue a General Order prohibiting the further use of this favorite bread as an article of food by the soldiers, and having it adopted by the Ordnance Department as a more effective missile fired from a cannon than the famous conical ball now so popular with the artillery. I know these same 'dodgers' have contributed more to thin the ranks of the 36th Regiment than the enemy. The 'pones,' which are a decided improvement, are fashioned like our old wheaten loaves and from their peculiar shape and hardness are termed by the boys 'grindstones.' They answer a very good purpose: to set their teeth on edge. There is another article produced here, though not to as great an extent as those before–mentioned. I allude to the dried apple pies. To give you just an idea of them, I would say that two circular pieces of leather, fresh and undried, sewed together at the edges and stuffed with pumice from a cider press, resemble our Virginia pies more than anything else I can think of. Why only the other day I saw two fellows batting each other over the head with these same 'sole–leather' pies, and it was evident to all that the boys were damaged more than the pies.

"I had my likeness taken yesterday which will send with this," Pvt. Hechler wrote his sister. "The one in the smallest case I want you to give to Cousin Hannah. We have had one picture taken with John and me in one case. You may keep that one if you choose."

WRITING IN MAY 2, 1862, Pvt. Hechler happily reported that the routine had changed somewhat as the time to break camp approached:

> We have only four hours drill now in a day. If the weather is favorable it is devoted to one hour battalion drill, commencing 6:30 a.m. in the forenoon; company drill at 8:30 a.m. and skirmish drill in the afternoon. So you see we have about half the time for ourselves besides roll call and dress parade, but are required to be ready in our quarters any minute if called on. We had a general inspection and muster on day before yesterday, and the Colonel (Crook) inspected closely and found many faults.
>
> So there are now two more months' wages due us. Perhaps

the paymaster will be around soon again. I do not know how true it is that Captain Jewett Palmer has been appointed to General Fremont's staff, but I should not think it impossible.

I received the stamps and likeness you sent, and was very much pleased with the likeness. It is a tolerably good picture. You say you are lonely now, but do not get down-hearted. Cheer up and be thankful for the blessings you have, and probably with the will of God you will see your brothers again soon. Let us hope. I am not losesome here for my part, but often think about you and feel as though I would like to talk to you a little while. I guess Brother John is home wherever he strays!

There is a rumor in camp now that we will leave here soon. It is the general opinion of intelligent men here, besides officers who ought to know, that we will never be called into action, but if we should, you shall receive the news as quickly as possible, and all if it should come to the worst.

It is nearly time for roll-call, so I will close this letter by bidding you goodnight (There! I hear the drum now). And wishing you a sweet sleep, I still remain,

Your loving brother, George

JUST BEFORE LEAVING to take part in the battle of Lewisburg, Pvt. Hechler wrote to his sister in Marietta on May 11, 1862:

Have been out on another scout. I thought I would write a few lines this Sunday afternoon to let you know that I am still alive and well.

Well, we have had beautiful weather now all this month. Nights are cool but clear and the roads are now dry and dusty, so we had a more agreeable time on our scout than we had before. We started out Monday morning about daylight and came home yesterday afternoon, only marching three days in all and laying the rest of the time in an arcade waiting for some of the bushwhackers (or thieves) to come along. But only three made their appearance, and they received the punishment they deserved. Some of the other companies found several more. We had an easy time while lying concealed in the laurel thicket. Before long this will result in either killing all of them or they will stay home and attend to their business which latter would be a wise plan for them to adopt now, because in one more month the season for planting will be over, and if they do not raise anything starvation will certainly meet them.

There is some expectation of our moving from here soon to some other place in the neighborhood, as we shall not go far.

Yesterday evening, on dress parade, an order was read telling us that we now belonged to a new brigade composed of the 36th, 11th, 44th and 42nd regiments. Colonel George Crook is acting brigadier general. His duty will be to protect the Kanawha Valley. So we will scarcely see another engagement unless Floyd will make another attempt to get a little salt, but I think he will get pepper if he does.

John is well, but I shall close this letter.

I remain your loving brother, George

13. Ohio Troops Move to Engage Rebels

Quick Dash — Jackson River Depot Bridge

CHEERS RESOUNDED throughout Pvt. Hechler's camp in Summersville early in May, 1862, when definite orders were received to move out to engage the Rebels. At 4 a.m. on Monday, May 12, the regiment waded the Gauley River at Brock's Ferry, and then headed for Cold Knob, Frankford and Lewisburg on forced marches. Here is the way Pvt. Hechler described the journey in a letter to his faithful sister Kate in Marietta dated May 21, 1862:

My Dear Sister:

You will see by this letter, if you get it, that we have moved from Summersville. We started from there on the 12th, and came by the mountain route, having to go one man behind the other for a distance of over 40 miles, as the path was not wide enough for two to walk abreast. Colonel Crook walked ahead nearly all the way and gave his horse up to have knapsacks carried on it. The wagons took the road.

Wednesday, the 14th, we reached Frankford, 10 miles from Lewisburg, having travelled the distance of 60 miles in two days. We stayed till the next day, and then came to Lewisburg, but there was no rest for in the evening we were ordered to prepare five days' rations before lying down. On Friday morning we started for Jackson River Station, 40 miles from Lewisburg, where the enemy was said to be in force.

A considerable number was discovered about four miles from White Sulphur Springs, but they scattered and only one was taken. On the same evening one Captain Sprigg and 17 of

> his men were overtaken. This was thought to be a picket. The next day a small squad was seen running from a bridge that was built across Jackson River. One man was caught. He was too drunk to run. We reached the station at noon but found no enemy. Scoured the country for several miles around to where Jackson and Cow Pasture forms the James River, then returned and reached Lewisburg Monday evening, having been out for eight days. We marched for six of the eight days, and traveled 150 miles, making 25 miles per day.
>
> John and myself are both well. I shall close this letter, and let you know more particulars when I get them, and when I get rested a little. Do not believe any rumors, because there are a good many circulating.
>
> Bidding you good-by for awhile, I remain
> Your loving brother, George

THE QUICK DASH described by Pvt. Hechler in the above letter was actually of great strategic importance. The purpose of the drive was to cut the Virginia Central Railroad by destroying a railroad bridge ten miles to the east of Covington, and this the force succeeded in doing. Colonel Crook's well–trained 36th Ohio Volunteer Infantry Regiment joined with the 44th Ohio and 2nd West Virginia Cavalry Regiment to form a provisional brigade for the mission.

The same day that Pvt. Hechler was giving a "private's eye view" of the action in a letter to his sister, Major General John C. Fremont on May 21st was telegraphing a report on the same action to Secretary of War Stanton. General Fremont's report:

> Colonel Crook, commanding brigade in Greenbrier County has just returned from a successful dash upon the Central Railroad, 10 miles beyond Covington, at Jackson's River Depot. Dispatches were discovered at the telegraph office in Covington from the provost- marshal of Alleghany County, asking General Jackson,

Major-General Henry Heth, C.S.A.

at Staunton, for two or three regiments and stating that he was endeavoring to raise the militia of Greenbrier and Monroe. Answers were also found promising reinforcements from Jackson by way of Staunton and from General Floyd by way of Sweet Springs. To prevent any immediate advance from Staunton, Colonel Crook proceeded from Covington, destroyed the railroad bridge 10 miles in advance of that place, and returned to Callaghan's thence to Lewisburg, bringing with him the notorious Captain Sprigg and another guerrilla, captured after firing upon our troops.

J. C. Fremont, Major-General

LOOKING AT THE OTHER SIDE of the picture, here is how the Confederate Army viewed the action of Pvt. Hechler's unit in destroying the Jackson River Depot bridge, revealed in a dispatch dated May 20, 1862 from Confederate Lt. Col. W. H. Werth to Major-General W. W. Loring:

> Knowing General Heth's movements, I hasten to give you the following facts, just to hand:
>
> The telegraphic operator, with his papers, at Jackson River was captured by the enemy. Among the undestroyed dispatches was one ordering two of Jackson's regiments and Ashby's cavalry to the rear of the enemy at Covington. As soon as captured, the enemy fell back to Lewisburg. At the latter post he has been strongly reinforced within the last thirty-six hours.
>
> If Heth makes the contemplated move, he may easily be seriously threatened and annoyed by a superior force on his left.
>
> The enemy burned the first railroad bridge between Jackson River Depot.
>
> General Cox's headquarters are at Lewisburg. The operator was making his way off with his instruments, etc., when he was captured. I think this information is entirely reliable.

Actually, Pvt. Hechler's unit had moved with super speed as to take the Rebels by surprise. Thus the Confederate forces were not given sufficient time to mobilize the troops with which they could easily have inflicted a serious defeat on the Union troops in the mountains.

Confederate General Henry Heth, fresh from a smashing victory over General Cox near Princeton at Giles Court-house early in May, now coiled his forces at Salt Sulphur Springs for an assault on Lewisburg. With a much smaller force at Lewisburg, Pvt. Hechler's regiment braced itself for the blow they did not know when to expect.

14. Battle of Lewisburg

Attractive Town in a Hollow — Breakfast Attack
Marietta Report — Battle was Brief — Watched Enemy

LEWISBURG, THE COUNTY SEAT of Greenbrier County, was the point where General Andrew Lewis mobilized his forces to march forward to the Battle of Pt. Pleasant. During the Civil War, Lewisburg was a strategic point commanding the Kanawha Valley, and in the spring of 1862 Confederate General Henry Heth sent a force of 3,000 to cut off Pvt. Hechler's regiment—which had made a daring dash 10 miles beyond Covington to destroy a railroad bridge on the Jackson River.

Colonel George Crook, hearing that General Heth was trying to slash his overextended lines, pulled back to Lewisburg, where the 26th and 44th Ohio regiments joined 200 men of the 2nd West Virginia Cavalry Regiment to defend this attractive town in a hollow surrounded by hills.

"I shall try and tell you a little about the battle of Lewisburg," Hechler wrote to his sister on June 3, 1862. "On the morning of the 23rd, at dawn, the pickets at Greenbrier Bridge were driven in, but only the Confederate cavalry could come through. Their infantry had to hide in the woods and some were taken prisoner."

> We had just gotten up when our captain came around and told us to get into ranks with arms only, and then we knew there would be something to do. We started out double-quick. Co. D of the 44th was ahead of us. We went through town and up the hill, out of town on the upper side, deceived by the fog. We came

across a group on the road thinking they were our pickets, and we came within less than 100 yards of them only to be met by a sharp volley. Most of them were concealed behind a small house surrounded by shade trees and shrubberies behind fences, and lying in the tall grass. We were ordered to lie down until two sharp volleys were sent over us, some of the balls disagreeably close to our heads, throwing up dirt around us. Now they stopped, thinking thy had us all killed, but what was their surprise when we all jumped up and commenced retreating and firing!

We formed a line again, and waited in town for further orders. They now commenced a furious cannonading, with one and then increased to eight pieces of artillery. They did some wild shooting. Before commencing to bombard us, they had raised a shout, calling: "Lewisburg is ours!"

Colonel Crook now rode ahead toward the enemy to ascertain his position. He soon came back and ordered the 36th to the left and the 44th to the right, where most of the artillery was stationed supported only by a few hundred militia. We formed a line of battle under the fire of the enemy, but behind a small rise. We now started forward, and as we gained the crest of the rise the Rebels were seen standing in line ready to receive us—three Regiments of them. A shout rolled down our line, but the Rebels did not fire, the distance yet being too great for them. When within about 150 yards of them we were commanded to halt. They had saved this opportunity to deliver their fire, and we were not slow to reply. After a few rounds, the enemy fled in confusion and in every direction, leaving behind cartridge belts, some with the belts cut, guns, horses, sacks with a little ration in some, biscuits, canteens, overcoats, blankets, drawers, pants, vests, shorts and other articles strewn along the road.

We did not follow too far on account of the ground being very rough and hilly, slipping toward the Greenbrier River. Two companies were deployed as skirmishers and followed the retreating Rebels to Greenbrier Bridge, which was found to be in flames. We then returned to camp but I had to go on picket duty. So I had to wait for my breakfast till we were at our post when we built a fire, cooked some coffee, and ate a hearty breakfast which done also for dinner.

There were many rumors, first concerning our losses, but Col. Crook's official report, as read on dress parade, congratulating the troops, settled all doubt of it. You have seen it in the papers, but there is some difference there. We captured four cannon, 300 stand of small arms, over 100 prisoners that had not been wounded, and the enemy left over 100 dead and wounded on the battlefield. Our loss was 44 killed, 53 wounded, 2 or 3 mortal. All the rest were getting along well at last accounts. Nearly all were sent to Charleston, or on further, to be taken care of.

After the battle we saw more of the inhabitants than we had before, especially women. Some came to hunt up husbands, other brothers and friends. Alas, only too many found the lost dead, wounded or taken prisoner. Some of them showed remarkable intelligence and knowledge, but others are rough and almost ignorant. (I speak of the women for the men are nearly all gone.)

We are camped here now on a bluff, the sides are not too steep but gently sloping. The camp had the appearance of a grove, but we had to clear out the underbrush so it looks more like a clearing when on it. We have no tents but had to build bunks, spreading our guns with blankets over them for a roof. A roof is needed now, for it has been raining for the greater part of three days. Sunday we had two heavy hail storms.

General Heth, who commanded the Rebel forces, had promised his men a good breakfast in Lewisburg—this was reported by prisoners, who confirmed on searching the houses for arms after the battle, as many had biscuits, pie and bread baked in large quantities, meat and other things cooked up.

If Heth should resolve to eat another breakfast in our tavern we shall have the coffee at least warm enough for him.

I shall have to close this letter now, hoping it will find you well, I remain,

Your loving brother, GEORGE

Lt. Col. Melvin Clarke, who took command of the 36th regiment when Col. Crook was promoted to become a brigade commander, had this to say in his official report the day after the battle of Lewisburg: "Though the first battle in which the regiment was ever engaged, the men behaved nobly. From the time we arrived beyond the houses we had to pass and received the first fire of the enemy, the battalion pressed steadily and firmly forward in the face of the galling fire. Not a man flinched. The steadiness, firmness, determination and vigor with which the line moved on, together with the rapidity and accuracy of our fire, seemed to inspire the enemy-though twice our number or more-with terror."

What did General Heth, the Confederate commander have to say about the Battle of Lewisburg? Did he share Pvt. Hechler's view that this was a great Union victory? Here is what General Heth reported to his superiors:

> I proceeded rapidly in the direction of Lewisburg. I had the most accurate information of the enemy's force in every respect. My chances of success were good, provided I could surprise the enemy and get into position. This I succeeded in doing far beyond my expectation. Most of his pickets were captured, and I attained without firing a shot that position in front of Lewisburg which I would have selected... The enemy, numbering only three companies, opened a very severe fire, which possibly compelled the command to fall back. At this time the left of the enemy was in full retreat. One of those causeless panics for which there is no accounting seized upon my command. Victory was in my grasp, instead of which I have to admit a most disgraceful retreat.

The long, dull days of drill and discipline for Pvt. Hechler's regiment had paid off in its baptism of fire. Perhaps the best commentary came from Colonel George Crook, the West Pointer who had trained the 36th: "This was the first time my regiment was under fire, but old veterans could not have done better, for a more handsome victory was not gained during the war."

AS PVT. GEORGE HECHLER REMINISCED about the Battle of Lewisburg, the first battle of the Civil War in which he had fought, he marveled that everything seemed to go right for his regiment and the Union forces. He had not even finished his breakfast on the morning of May 23, 1862, when the Union pickets were driven in and the force of 3,000 picked men under Confederate General Henry Heth attacked Lewisburg, which was defended by only 1,200 soldiers of the Union.

Pvt. Hechler checked his watch when the excitement started: it was one minute after 5 A.M. At the southern border of Lewisburg was a ridge commanding the town, and General Heth took possession of this strategic ridge. Hechler and his buddies took cover as best they could in the streets of the town, lying on sidewalks and paved streets. The Rebels ran up two big cannon and started to unlimber them, and "then we could see them coming over the ridge like grasshoppers in a stubblefield," one of Hechlers's fellow soldiers reported. Men, women and children of Lewisburg scurried for cover as the Confederates poured grape, canister and shell into the town, and Hechler's company fell back to the center of town.

Now suddenly the newly made Brigadier General George Crook appeared. He rode up and ordered Hechler's company to advance. Marietta's Captain Jewett Palmer, the company commander, sounded the command: "Company G as skirmishers on the right file—take intervals—double-quick, MARCH!"

Somehow the months of training, the agonizing waits, the cold and rainy weather all seemed worthwhile now as the men reacted instinctively. They advanced, fired, dropped down, re-loaded, raised up, fired again, and continued to advance at a double-quick pace.

THE MARIETTA HOME NEWS issue of June 13, 1862, reporting on the great victory at Lewisburg, noted: "The 36th and 44th regiments have immortalized themselves. It was certainly one of the best fought battles and greatest victory that has yet been achieved during the war, and our boys are 'shouting happy'. They say we have been spoiling all winter for a fight, and have got it at last; and nobly did they sustain the character of brave men. The odds were all against us: six pieces of heavy artillery in position, and 3,000 men, against 1,200. They were commanded by one of their ablest men, General Heth, and had the 22nd Regiment, their brag regiment, pitted against the 36th. They say they have been in four fights, and were never whipped, but they woke up the wrong passengers this time. Our men never gave way an inch, but kept pressing steadily forward, until the Rebels broke in the utmost confusion. Then such a shout went up from our boys as you never heard."

After the battle, one of Pvt. Hechler's regimental officers, Captain William A. Walden, wrote this to his wife on May 28, 1862: "I talked with one of the Confederate lieutenants who was shot through the arm and later captured. He said that they had been in nearly every battle in West Virginia, including Scary Creek, Cross Lanes and Carnifex Ferry, and they had confidently expected to whip us."

IN A FEW HOURS the battle was over, and by 7:30 A.M. Pvt. Hechler was back in camp eating a hearty breakfast. He ruefully observed that mounting of the guard took place promptly at 9 a.m. as it did every day, just as though nothing had happened. On the 29th of May at 8 a.m., the command "Fall in!" echoed throughout camp and the 36th Ohio Volunteer Infantry Regiment set out along dusty roads for the march to Meadow Bluff. Here is Pvt. Hechler's account in a letter of May 31 to his sister Kate in Marietta:

My Dear Sister:

I shall try and write you a few lines this forenoon here in our new camp at Meadow Bluff. We left Lewisburg on the 29th, coming to here 15 miles northwest. This we consider a retreat, but there had been no enemy near and we could do it at leisure on account of the victory which, by the grace of God, we gained at Lewisburg. The Union cause has gained some strength here in this part of Virginia, but the dying Monster Secesh may struggle hard yet and give us some hard blows if not properly taken care of.

We are now 55 miles farther from Richmond that we were at Jackson Station, and are advanced as far as the rest of our lines. Yesterday, we had the underbrush to clear off for several hundred yards wide, so now we have a pleasant grove for a camping ground, on the crest of the hill. There are numerous rumors here about the enemy approaching, but if he attacks us here we shall at least have our own chosen position and we hope, with the help of God, to defeat them again. Our force is not very large, but much larger than at the Battle of Lewisburg, for we have now 10 pieces of artillery and a regiment of infantry.

I do not believe that Heth will make another such a dashing attack, for fear of being taken at his own game, but he will push slowly forward to meet us. We have heard some splendid news lately, but do not get it often here in the wilderness.

I have not received a letter from you for a long time, and do not know what is the reason. We shall have to drill this afternoon, so I shall have to close these few lines by wishing you good-bye 'till I find another time to write, John and myself are both well yet.

Remember your brother, George

THERE FOLLOWED FOR PVT. HECHLER and his regiment a summer of comparative inactivity following the hard fight at Lewisburg. They bivouacked between two swamps at Meadow Bluff, mainly watching the enemy and making an occasional dash across the Greenbrier River into that rich garden around Union and Salt Sulphur Springs. On June 15, 1862, Pvt. Hechler wrote to his sister Kate:

My Dear Sister:

I thought I would write a few lines to you this beautiful and warm Sunday morning, as I will have a good chance to send a letter by our quartermaster, Mr. Barber. He told me yesterday evening he was going to start home today or tomorrow, and offered to take a letter for me. He is very kind and attentive to me, and tells me whenever he gets a letter from home where you name is mentioned.

We are yet encamped here on the bluff where we came from Lewisburg. The 44th has built breastworks along their front and flanks, but we have not done anything yet, and scarcely will. There is a small Rebel force 25 miles from here, and the scouting parties, mostly cavalry, frequently meet, most always with loss to the Rebels. We have four or five now captured in that way, and some were killed. Our Cavalry lost one man, supposed to be wounded and made a prisoner.

When the news of Stonewall Jackson's advance first reached camp it was feared he would threaten our rear, but while we have such commanders as Fremont, and Crook we need not fear. They both possess the entire confidence of the men. Cox is frequently compared by the men in this Brigade (and we belong to his Division) with his father-in-law, the Rebel General John B. Floyd, running at every opportunity presented, but it may not all be his fault.

Camp is dull at present, not even many rumors, because every evening on dress parade the telegraphic dispatches are read to us as received at headquarters, so there is not much room for speculation in regard to victories and defeats. There is at present no prospect of quiet being disturbed soon here at this place, but it would be better for us if soon, for the sick list is increasing fast. But there are no serious cases. The most, I think, are caused by change of water and food. We draw about three fourths of the meat since we came here in fresh beef, and have had pork all winter and spring, but with few exceptions.

The paymaster was here last week and paid off the 44th and the 47th, but not the 36th. I do not know what is the reason, but it is said he had not enough money. "There will be four months' wages due us by the first of next month, and we will hardly be paid off before that time.

If you have a chance, when Mr. Barber comes back, send me a pair of socks.

We are both (John and I) enjoying good health yet, and I hope you are the same.

The slowness of the Potomac Army is not liked much here, and if McClellan does not soon move faster he will lose his reputation as a Commander, even among the soldiers, not only among Army correspondents and newspaper writers. I saw a letter in camp from Thomas, dated only one day later than yours, stating that a dispatch had been received which said the 36th was cut all to pieces at Lewisburg, and the writer of the letter appeared to believe it and was much excited about it. This is certainly corrected before this time, but I hope if such rumors reach you, you will not believe them or trouble yourself about them until you know the truth, which you will always find out soon enough.

The correspondent of the Marietta Home News, signed W.S.S., from the 36th, is the most reliable of all public correspondents written from the regiment. The writer was a member of our Company G, but is now Sergeant Major.

I do not think the war can last much longer unless the Rebels adopt a guerrilla warfare which would certainly result in their speedy annihilation, especially in this department. They are nearly settled now, or else the name of Fremont holds them in check. All the Secesh in this country appear to fear him.

The sky is clouding up and the wind is rising as the sun does, and we shall have a shower, perhaps before tonight. Inspection is just over and the Captain was satisfied with all, but one exception. We have company inspection every Sunday morning at 6:00 o'clock.

I shall have to close this letter now.

Bidding you goodbye, I remain,

Your loving brother, George.

As the warm weather came, the first full summer which George and John Hechler had spent away from their Ohio Valley home, they became a little more restless-never admitting they were homesick. John Hechler, the happy-go-lucky member of the family, did not feel it as keenly as George. Little did they expect that within a few months they would be back in Parkersburg and Marietta. Nor did they anticipate that they would spend the winter in the Kanawha Valley in the vicinity of Charleston.

15. Expedition to Salt Sulphur Springs

Gen. Crook Shares Stretegy — Camped on Summit

WAR ALWAYS LOOKS DIFFERENT to a private in the infantry, trying his best to figure out the "big picture" but always suspecting that the officers are holding out something on him. The success of General George Crook was his ability to communicate, in a quiet way, so everybody in his units saw the big picture.

Flushed with their first battle victory at Lewisburg, Pvt. Hechler and the 36th Regiment restlessly wanted to press forward. Pvt. Hechler could not control his disappointment when the 36th was forced to retreat to Meadow Bluff. General Crook knew the mood of his men, itching for action to hurry the end of the war. But he also knew that a general named Stonewall Jackson was poised and ready to cut off his line of retreat if he stuck his neck out too far.

The Rebel forces were concentrated across the Greenbrier River near Salt Sulphur Springs and Union in Monroe County. General Crook decided to send some of his picked men, including Pvt. Hechler's Company G of the 36th, in a forced march over rough, rocky territory to strike a surprise blow. It was one of the most rugged and wearing marches Hechler had ever experienced, the entire first night covering 20 miles over rocky peaks, along a narrow path that could only be identified by the rattling of leaves underfoot when the men left the path.

Here is how Pvt. Hechler described the expedition to Salt Sulphur Springs in a letter to his sister Kate, dated June 27, 1862:

Major-General Jacob D. Cox

My Dear Sister:

I shall write you a few lines this afternoon, although I do feel very tired yet and do not much feel like writing.

The weather is very hot and the ground is getting dry. Even the springs about our camp are getting so low that we are obliged to dip the water with a tin cup into the bucket, and sometimes wait till it comes out of the vein first, and when we do get it, it is not very clear.

Last Friday afternoon we received orders to prepare four days' rations and roll our blankets ready to start at a minute's warning, but Saturday morning came on and wore away without any start. The reason for this was transportation. Our teams with the bread did not come as soon as expected, and there was only two days' rations in camp.

Saturday evening, as expected, two companies, D and G of the 36th, under command of Captain Palmer, started, we know not where for, but we travelled all night over the mountains till about daylight when we reached Greenbrier River and forded it. We then made our way through the woods to the Union or

Salt Sulphur Road for the purpose of capturing a picket post stationed on the road near the regular crossing place. But they had heard of our move and withdrawn the day before, so we only succeeded in capturing a few bushwhackers, one artilleryman and one cavalryman. The artilleryman had been in the fight at Lewisburg and had done some close shooting at the camp.

Through a mistake, one of our own cavalrymen was mortally wounded Sunday afternoon. Monday, bushwhackers fired on us several times, wounding two men, one only slightly in the face.

Tuesday morning about eight o'clock we came to Salt Sulphur Springs, but the enemy had gone and we were obliged to come back to camp again without meeting the man we had become a little acquainted with at Lewisburg (General Heth.) Some of our boys did not think him very manly but we still found a little for our trouble, for we found some small arms, mostly muskets, fifteen or twenty We came back to camp Wednesday afternoon, sore and tired. At the town of Union and along the road we heard that General Heth carried away over 100 women, and some dead. His troops are so demoralized that the name of Crook and the 36th Regiment is enough to raise an excitement in their camp any time, as contrabands say who came in with us.

The country is the best grazing ground I have yet seen anywhere. There is plenty of water, but scarcely any creek is a half-mile long till it disappears again under the mountain.

Crops generally look well, but are much later than in Ohio.

I shall have to close this letter as I am getting tired. Write soon.

Remember your loving brother, George

It was an unblazed and trackless wilderness through which Pvt. Hechler and the Union troops made their forced march, pushing through almost impenetrable thickets of laurel. They did achieve some surprise, such as capturing the guards who, not dreaming there was any danger, were skylarking a little at the Greenbrier River crossing at Alderson's Ferry. By the sudden dash, General Crook also wanted to stop the stripping of the countryside of forage and the impressment of many civilians into Confederate service. But Pvt. Hechler and his regiment finally had to concede the superior fleetfootedness of the troops they had nicknamed the "Fast-Fleeing Virginians" who eluded their grasp.

And so it was back to Meadow Bluff, and up to a camp on the summit of the Alleghenies where even with long military overcoats and woolen underwear it was still chilly on July 2nd, Fourth of July, 1862. Hechler's first Independence Day away from home was a wonderful memory. The 22-year old infantryman spent the morning gathering cherries and Juneberries. It was not a chilly and comfortable pleasant, 36 rounds fired from rifled Parrott guns constituted the only demonstration in camp.

Rumors began to circulate freely again during the period of skirmishing, scouting and lack of movement. In General Crook's camp, gossip had it that the division commander, General Jacob D. Cox, took a dim view of Crook's sudden dash to Salt Sulphur Springs. This might explain some remarks Pvt. Hechler made in his July 14, 1862 letter:

> My Dear Sister:
>
> I shall try and write you a few lines today to let you know that we are well yet at present, and I hope they will find you well and your hand all right. I have not had any chance yet of talking to Mr. Barber since he came back.
>
> I received the socks you sent and was very glad I got them because Government socks always make my feet sore on a march.
>
> We have very fine weather here now. The nights are cool and days nearly all the time. A fresh breeze is stirring the leaves. All the work we have to do is to have drill each day, Sunday excepted, and dress parade in the evening.

We have 6 more escaped prisoners now in the guard-house. Three of them were brought in today and three last Saturday. We have scouting parties out now day and night, but have not lost any man or horse yet in wounded or killed, or prisoners. All of them expect that the Confederate flag will wave over Meadow Bluff in less than two weeks. Appearances would point to the possibility of an attack, as they advance their pickets slowly toward us, and guerillas have been seen within about four miles of our camp, although I think they will not think the neighborhood very healthy long.

Captain Palmer is Officer of the Day again today. He was before the Battle of Lewisburg. There's some say Cox has fallen back, others he had advanced. I do not know which he had done. His force is said to be 10,000; ours is scarcely three, and we might possibly get reinforcement before the Rebels could bring on an engagement, but we do not care much. Every man has full confidence in General Crook, our commander, and is willing to follow him, so with the help of God we expect to gain a victory if we have to fight.

One of the prisoners was a citizen and Prosecuting Attorney of Guyandotte, Virginia, before the war broke out, and is well known to some of the boys in our regiment.

Write soon if you can, and tell me how all the folks are getting along. I shall have to close now because I don't know any more to write, give my love to all enquiring folks and tell them not to forget me.

I remain, your loving brother, George.

16. The Dog Days of 1862

July Fades Into August — Gen. Pope Takes Over
Wanted Fight — Busted to Private

THE HOT AND DUSTY DAYS of July were succeeded by cool nights in the Greenbrier Valley "They tell me we'll be moving back to Charleston and Parkersburg soon," one of the 36th Ohio Regiment told Pvt. Hechler as July, 1862 faded into August.

Something had to happen soon. The Confederates were being reinforced strongly along the Greenbrier River. Through petty raids they were harassing Hechler's regiment, killing a few, wounding some, and taking prisoners in night raids. There was a let-down in discipline after the Battle of Lewisburg, and when daily squad drill every forenoon was ordered, Pvt. Hechler rejoiced. He and others felt that some soldiers were getting too loose and careless in ranks.

Perhaps this was the reason why a thorough general review and inspection of the 36th was held on the 1st of August. Then came a drawing of several days' rations on August 4, and at 5 P.M. the regiment set out from Meadow Bluff with the intention of routing two Rebel regiments beyond the Greenbrier River. They marched until 4 am when they were directed into a dense wood.

"Lie down, keep quiet and don't build any fires," were the orders which Pvt. Hechler received. He looked around in the early morning haze and could barely make out a grove of densely growing young chestnut trees. Finally about 9 in the morning, the men were allowed to build fires and eat. It was a hearty breakfast, apples, peaches, pears, onions, light bread, milk, butter and crackers—and they ate off and on all day. Then they were off again 8:30 p.m. marching over rough roads, through forests and creeks, until 1 a.m. when they were halted in a thick growth of underbrush. The men were kept awake all night, the officers poking the sleepers, and then in the morning they were ordered back into ranks and marched back to Meadow Bluff.

As one of Hechler's G Company put it: "We were told we had accomplished our mission but what it is we know not."

Had the young brothers George and John Hechler known that Parkersburg and Marietta were less than two weeks away, they would have faced all the confusion with light-hearted gaiety. Little did they know that the confusion had its source in the highest command of the Union Army.

AT THE END OF JUNE, 1862, President Lincoln, irked with the slowness of General McClellan, ordered Major General John Pope to take over the Army of Virginia, including the forces under General Fremont, whose Mountain Department was abolished. General J. D. Cox, commanding the "Kanawha Division" of which Col. Crook and Hechler's regiment were a part, telegraphed General Pope on July 3, 1862: "In view of the report that disciplined troops are wanted in the East, I call your attention to the fact that my division is among the best-seasoned and oldest troops in the field and with discipline and drill will compare favorably with any. We are desirous of joining the principal column, especially if the work here for a time is to be that of garrisoning the country, as it probably must be."

General Pope replied, dead-pan, five days later in a telegram to General Cox: "Do you think by leaving 2,500 men, with battery of artillery, strongly entrenched at or near mouth of Gauley, the valley of the Kanawha will be reasonably safe, if so, with what force will you be able to march on Staunton? How long will it take you to get there, and what resistance are you likely to meet?"

MAJOR GENERAL JOHN POPE

GENERAL COX SENT two more telegrams urging the same suggestion he had made in his July 3 message, and dead-panned back to his superior: "Nothing from you since my Nos. 4 and 5 were sent. Fearsome miscarriage of dispatches." (This translated, meant "For crying out loud, let me know when my boys can join the fight!")

Pope now started to get into an argument with Chief of Staff Halleck as to the best way to proceed. When it all got ironed out, Pope ordered Cox to march by way of Lewisburg, and Covington to Harrisonburg. General Cox pointed out, in protest, that the march would take fifteen days of uninterrupted marching through a mountainous region most of it in a wilderness destitute of supplies, and with the enemy upon the flank.

Why not, General Cox asked, march to Charleston, board steamers down the Kanawha River to Point Pleasant, thence up the Ohio River to Parkersburg, and then take the Baltimore and Ohio Railroad to Washington, D.C.? General Cox estimated this would take 10 days instead of the hazardous fifteen by the other plan. Pope finally consented to the plan, and ordered General Cox to leave 5,000 men in West Virginia and send the others to Washington, D.C. by river to Parkersburg and thence by rail.

And so August 14 was a happy day for the Hechler brothers. They received the news that they were bound for Parkersburg and home!

THE DAY WAS NOT SO HAPPY for every member of Hechler's company. For example, there was Sgt. John T. Booth of Company G, one of Hechler's close friends who was "busted" to private and thrown into the brig. He was charged with calling his company commander a "damned fool." Colonel Crook took a personal interest in Booth's case, and according to Booth's diary entry of August 14:

> Col. Crook called me in about five o'clock this evening. He scolded me out and hard. I never had such a lecture on military ethics in my life. It was straight brief and a pointed and sharp as a two-edged sword. He did not spare my feelings one particle. Before sending me away he advised that thereafter I be respectful and obedient to my superiors.

Sgt. Booth told Pvt. Hechler that he was mortified with the prospect of having his family come to Parkersburg and see him under guard, "We are going to Parkersburg," Sgt. Booth said. "there will be my father, mother, sisters and brothers. You may take my body as clay, but in the flesh will not be taken to Parkersburg as a prisoner." (Later, by special direction of Col. Crook, Sgt. Booth was freed when it was clear he had learned his lesson.)

The march to Charleston started on the 15th of August, the troops arrived at the top of Little Sewell Mountain at 9 a.m. and had a chance to gaze at the Rebel fortifications of Generals Floyd and Wise. They reached Big Sewell Mountain at 11:30 a.m. Onward they pressed. And from Gauley Bridge, General Cox sent the following telegram to the Quartermaster General on August 16, 1862:

> By command of Major General Pope I notify you that I shall be at Parkersburg on the evening of the 20th, with 5,000 infantry, two batteries of six guns each, 300 cavalry, and the camp equipage and regimental trains complete going to join General Pope Railroad transportation will be needed for, say, 1,100 animals-including everything, 270 wagons. Please inform me what arrangements will be made and how far I go by rail.

17. Return To Parkersburg

Jewett Palmer — Glided Into Ohio — Reminded of Home

COMPANY G of the 36th Ohio Volunteer Infantry was a rollicking collection of diverse humanity, disciplined in battle, full of pranks on the march, uncontrollably rowdy in the barracks. This weird collection of different characters was held together by a young, sharp Marietta attorney named Jewett Palmer (who later served several terms as mayor of Marietta).

In the summer of 1862, after the battle of Lewisburg, Palmer contracted typhoid fever. While his men were marching through the dense underbrush from Greenbrier County to Charleston, Captain Palmer bounced along the rough mountain roads in a horse-drawn ambulance. Pvt. Hechler's company suffered from Captain Palmer's absence. Lt. James Stanley and Lt. Homer Cherrington tried to hold the company together as the command passed back and forth between them.

On August 17, 1862, the company arrived at Lover's Leap and Hawk's Nest. Hechler gazed down below where the New River wound like a silver thread through the canyons. It was a sight of sobering grandeur. But after a short pause, the company pressed onward toward Charleston and arrived at "Camp Piatt" outside of Charleston at 5 p.m. There they had a chance for a bath and a swim in the Kanawha River. Since the bath and swim took place 148 years ago, it was probably accurate when one of Hechler's buddies wrote in his diary that "the water was clear and bright, of about the temperature to prove pleasant and inviting."

James Stanley

Homer C. Cherrington

At 9 A.M. on August 18, the men boarded a large stern-wheel steamer named the *Allen Collier* and two smaller steamers, named the *General Meigs* and the *General Pike*. The steamers slipped cable and went out into mid-stream, pausing opposite Charleston in midmorning to pick up Captain Palmer and the other convalescents who had made the trip by wagon over the mountains. At noon, they passed Scary Creek, scene of Albert Gallatin Jenkins' Confederate victory over the Union forces the year before.

It was about 4 o'clock in the afternoon when the steamers reached the mouth of the Kanawha River at Pt. Pleasant. Cheers and laughter arose from Hechler's company when the band struck up a current popular tune "Out of the Wilderness." The number by the band seemed very appropriate to the men as they glided into the waters of the Ohio River after having been "in the wilderness" for so many months.

As the troops headed up the Ohio River from Pt. Pleasant to Parkersburg, the news spread like wildfire that the entire Kanawha

Division was on its way to the Rapidan to join General Pope's army. The entire move planned and executed troop movements during the Civil War. All details were carefully mapped out and planned. The troops started on time, made their rendezvous at prescribed times, boarded the steamers on time, and the steamers moved out on time. This was a far cry from the "hurry up and wait" fare the Army customarily dished out to its men.

On the night of August 18, the steamers lay off Mason City until nearly midnight, then took a chance on the low water and only steamed upstream about five minutes before they were grounded. There they lay on the mud until 9 the next morning when some of the troops were ordered ashore to lighten the boat.

Sgt. John Booth (later a prominent Cincinnati physician) and Austin Bell, along with several others in Company G took the yawl across to Racine where the gang assembled at Austin Bell's uncle's house for breakfast. While there, Austin's uncle pointed to a white cottage on the Mason county side and exclaimed to Sgt. Booth: "John, one of your boyhood sweethearts, Irma Kern—now Mrs. Irma Paden—lives over there in that cottage!" And so the boys crossed the river to pay a call on Irma, who brought out a pitcher of milk and a pie. But oh, the disillusionment when they discovered Irma had developed into a rank Rebel, and had named her little daughter "Caroline Beauregard."

DURING THE AFTERNOON, while the steamers came to a dead stop below Buffington's Island, Hechler and his buddies discovered quite a bevy of maidens fair dressed in their Sunday best. It seems that there was to be a wedding in the village church. Somebody did a little fast thinking and organizing and procured the regimental flag. Then the men in blue from Company G fell in and marched to the home of the bride. Discreet inquiries revealed that their presence would be most welcome, so the company in full dress uniform fell in with drums beating and the fifes playing, and escorted the bride and groom to church. The ceremony was just what the Union boys needed to remind them of home and hearth, after being cooped up in the mountain fastnesses for a year.

Then it was back on the steamers again, and another attempt to move. General Jacob D. Cox, commanding the movement described the difficulties this way: "At Letart Falls, on the Ohio, the water was a broken rapid, up which the boats had to be warped one at a time, by means of a heavy warp—line made fast to the bank and carried to the steam—capstan on the steamer. At the foot of Blennerhassett Island there was only two feet of water in the channel, and the boats dragged themselves over the bottom by 'sparring' a process somewhat like an invalid's pushing a wheelchair along by a pair of crutches."

When Hechler's company reached Blennerhassett Island, further progress seemed impossible, so the whole regiment debarked at 5 p.m. and marched six miles up to Belpre. From there, they took a ferry and finally reached Parkersburg as dusk was falling.

18. Crowd Greets Soldiers in Parkersburg

Muster and Parade — New Recruits
Stopped at Clarksburg

NEARLY A YEAR HAD PASSED since George and his brother John Hechler had signed up for their three-year hitch in the Union Army. Now, on a hot August evening in 1862, they were coming home again. When they reached Parkersburg, a tremendous crowd of friends and relatives was on hand to greet the boys in blue. Not only did the people of Parkersburg turn out in force, but it seemed as though the entire population of Marietta was waiting at the wharf too.

It was about 8 o'clock in the evening, and the gentle evening breezes were stirring, when the troops were ferried over to Parkersburg from Belpre. The tearful and joyful family reunions were cut short within a few hours, as the 36th Regiment was marched off to "Camp Union," across from the old Stephenson home near the Staunton and Northwestern turnpikes. At Camp Union, the regiment was joined by a group of new recruits to fill the ranks which had been thinned by battle and disease. The troops then received the following order:

Parkersburg, Virginia
August 20, 1862

The troops of this regiment will be mustered tomorrow morning at 8 o'clock A.M.

The muster will be preceded by a parade.

The men will appear on a parade in their dark blue uniforms.

> By Order of Col. George Crook, Commanding 36th Ohio Volunteer Infantry Regiment, Jonathan N. Parton, Adjutant.

The brothers Hechler did not have very much time to spend with their family, but they did manage to squeeze in a basket dinner with their Marietta visitors. George bought a new Army hat to celebrate the fact he had served for nearly a year. By the next morning he was to regret the cash outlay he made for the hat.

IT WAS 5 O'CLOCK in the afternoon of August 21, 1862, when the cry of "fall in!" came at Camp Union. Pvt. Hechler noticed that there were 11 new recruits in Co. G, as they marched through the cheering Parkersburg crowds to the B & O Railroad Station. At the station they had a chance to say some more good-byes and it was close to dark before the train started to move out slowly, with the home folks still clinging to the soldiers they could reach out and touch.

The night was warm and sticky with no breeze blowing. Hechler soon discovered that the troops were riding in stock cars with three seats placed in lengthwise, and 33 men to a car. Most of the men piled down in the cars and went to sleep soon after the train had passed Walker Station.

As the train rolled on toward Petroleum and Pennsboro, the heat became insufferable for Hechler, and the car also reeked of the odor of its former occupants (hogs). So he decided to climb up onto the roof. At first he watched the lights in the houses along the railroad as they swiftly flashed by. He wondered whether he would ever return to Parkersburg and Marietta. Then, to shield the flashing light from his eyes, he put his new hat over his face and fell fast asleep in the fresh night air.

AT DAYBREAK the troop train lurched to a stop on the outskirts of Clarksburg. Pvt. Hechler awoke suddenly. His new hat was gone, also his belt and canteen which had rolled off the top of the railroad car. He shook his head philosophically. This meant more papers to fill out, and some deductions from his next pay. But when he climbed down into the packed and smelly stock car below, he was still glad he had decided to sleep under the stars.

At Grafton, the train stopped to give everyone a chance to wash up and get a bite of breakfast. Then the train ground onward toward Cumberland, where they took aboard huge quantities of bread and apples to the delight of all the troops.

Hechler marveled at the kaleidoscopic, tumbling, sparkling waters of the Cheat River as the train hurtled onward. Going into Piedmont they added a second locomotive to push the load of humanity up the steep grade. It was a beautiful moonlight night, and many of Hechler's buddies climbed up to watch the breathtaking and historic Harpers Ferry gorge. But it was midnight, and Hechler himself missed it because he was asleep again, building up his strength for the nights when he knew he would have to march and fight and sleep amid shot and shell.

Enroute to join General Pope's army near Manassas, VA (Bull Run), the troop train pulled into Washington, D. C. about nine o'clock on Sunday morning, August 24th. Hechler got off to gaze at the scaffolding and unfinished Washington monument, and also the uncompleted Capitol. It gave him a feeling of confidence that President Abraham Lincoln had insisted that the work on the Capitol Building proceed during wartime, as this symbolized the determination of the President that the Union would endure.

The troops getting off the train at Washington were immediately met by smiling girls with baskets full of cakes, pies and sweetmeats. The boys were flattered by the attention, but soon discovered that these were not Red Cross girls with free goodies, and for soldiers who had not been paid for six months there were few who could afford the prices! Along about 2 o'clock in the afternoon, the order came to re-board the train cars. Sergeant Ward of Hechler's company remarked that the order came "without as much as an offer

Capt. Augustus T. Ward

to shake hands with the dignitaries or see the White House." There was a lot of grumbling talk about "wanting to see these Washington people who are living off my money and the money of the other taxpayers," but soon everybody was aboard for the trip across Long Bridge to Alexandria and out toward the ill-fated Second Battle of Bull Run.

19. The Second Battle of Bull Run

Bull Run Defeat — Railroad Cut
Encamped In Swamp — Impending Disaster

BULL RUN was a symbol of defeat for the Union Army, not only once, but twice.

In 1861, there was panic at Bull Run. In 1862, there was not as much panic, but the Union troops were clearly defeated.

It took nearly two months after the Second Bull Run defeat before Pvt. Hechler could bring himself to write home about it. Finally, on October 19, 1862, he penned a long letter to his sister in Marietta, reviewing what had happened since his happy home-coming in August. The letter postmarked Clarksburg started: "I have written but little since we left Parkersburg. I shall try and write you a little today about our journey from the time we left there 'til we came back to this place. We started from Parkersburg Sunday evening about eight o'clock . . . "

Everywhere after they crossed the Long Bridge into Alexandria Va., Hechler observed troops hurrying to the front and ambulances moving toward the rear. Near Manassas Junction, there were immense quantities of army stores piled high by the railroad tracks. The men could hear cannonading in the distance as they unloaded from their 80-hour-ride at Manassas. The first troops they saw were some Marietta boys in blue in the Pierpont Battery, West Virginia light artillery, who had been commanded by Frank Buell, killed a day or so before.

On August 25, the same day that Hechler arrived at Manassas Junction, a Confederate general named Stonewall Jackson swooped down and cut the railroad as he went into position behind General Pope's Army of the Potomac. This meant that Hechler's regiment, the 36th Ohio Volunteer Infantry, was the only regiment of the Kanawha Division to arrive for the Second Battle of Bull Run before Stonewall cut off the railroad.

General George Crook, who had trained and commanded the 36th regiment before turning it over to Lt. Col. Melvin Clarke of Marietta, was heartbroken that his favorite regiment might get lost in the shuffle. Years later, General Crook wrote in his autobiography:

> My regiment was 1,100 strong, and was the pride of my heart. I knew every man in it and had spent so much hard work on it, that I regarded it as one of my own family. I feared that we would be attached to some brigade that would take no interest in it, and feared being sacrificed, so I succeeded in getting detailed as bodyguard to General Pope's headquarters, and in this position went through the Second Battle of Bull Run.

At first, Hechler and his company were encamped in a huge swamp. They had to boil their water, which they reported included tadpoles and squirming vermin. Even on the eve of the battle, the new recruits were drilled. They even had time for a dress parade in the 36th Regiment, which so impressed General Hunter Strother of General Pope's staff, that he wrote: "In the afternoon, I went out to see the dress parade and drill of Col. Crook's famous regiment of infantry, the 36th Ohio, now on duty here as Headquarters Guard. This regiment, now nearly a thousand strong, went through its exercise with a precision I have never seen equaled."

Morale was high in Hechler's regiment, despite the rough living conditions.

Then that intrepid son of West Virginia, Stonewall Jackson

struck again. On August 26, Jackson captured Manassas Junction, General Pope's base of supplies, destroying 27 locomotives, 203 cars of provisions and other military stores. The whole northern horizon was red with burning warehouses and railroad trains. The conflagration was visible for forty miles in all directions, and caused great alarm in the nation's capital.

CROOK REPORTED:

> Although my position enabled me to see much that even a division commander in a large army could not, I could not get any comprehensive idea of how much that was going on. However, I shared the idea of all about me that some disaster was pending. Just before dusk on the evening our army fell back, 'Nosey' Ingalls of the Quartermaster Department came to me, and said: 'For God's sake draw up your men in line and stop the fugitives' He said that our army was badly beaten and many of the men were failing back in a rout, and unless stopped, they would not stop short of the Potomac. I did as he requested, and sure enough we must have caught ten or fifteen thousand men without organizations trying to get to the rear.

In his letter to his Marietta sister Kate, Pvt. Hechler reported:

> The next day a battle was fought in our rear and we had to commence falling back toward Washington. Three days afterward we reached Centerville, Va., where some prisoners came in and I was detailed to guard. Saturday when the news of our defeat came in, we were started off toward Washington, after night, about seven of us with 400 prisoners, some officers among them. We guarded them all night and marched to Alexandria the next day in the mud and the rain and confusion without anything to eat.

Two of Hechler's buddies in Company G, Sergeants Booth and Ward, recorded the misery in their diaries on August 30, 1862. Sgt.

Booth wrote: "It is now clearly evident the day is lost to us. Our forces are falling back on the right and on the left." Sgt. Ward, reporting that Company G was about to go on picket duty at Bull Run Bridge wrote on August 30: "It now becomes painfully evident that the Union Army is suffering a disastrous defeat."

All around there were the noises of war—the clatter of stamping and tramping of horses and mules, the rattling of thousands of wagons, the rumblings of the artillery, the clanking for cavalry sabers, the braying of thousands of irrepressible army mules, and the voices of a hundred thousand men-all blended together in a bewildering chorus.

This was the Second Battle of Bull Run.

In the White House, a tall, gaunt figure paced the floor of the presidential office.

Abraham Lincoln was still looking for a general.

20. White House Comedy

Saida Scott Writes — Lincoln Receives Governors Enjoyed Incident

THE SECOND BATTLE OF BULL RUN in 1862 marked the close of the first year of the Civil War.

Some of the frustration of the first year of war was expressed by a pretty and talented little girl from Marietta named Saida M. Scott, the daughter of a Marietta schoolmaster, Saida Scott was the sweetheart of Pvt. Hechler's company commander, Jewett Palmer. She wrote on September 6, 1862:

> Don't you think McClellan displays great generalship in his latest moves? I don't know whether you are an admirer of McClellan or not but you certainly must allow that we haven't many generals who after a year spent in marching and counter-marching would finally draw up in the very spot whence he started. After having killed off several thousand men and not having gained a decisive victory, I should be most decidedly a friend to Lincoln if he would only put Mac in some place where he could exercise his wonderful military genius without harming anyone but himself.

The same day that Saida Scott wrote from Marietta, Captain Palmer's company was marching through the nation's capital. The previous night they had camped on the lawn of the old Lee Homestead in Arlington, across the Potomac. After the Second Battle of Bull Run, Sgt. John Booth confided to his diary: "The fact is we are a badly whipped and practically demoralized army. The enemy is up to the gates of the capital knocking for admission." Despite this gloomy estimate, Hechler's regiment had actually performed an outstanding service in assembling stragglers and fugitives.

September 6, 1862 was a Saturday. Pvts. George and John Hechler marveled as they marched through Old Georgetown, past Francis Scott Key's house, and then with a swinging and steady stride down Pennsylvania Avenue to the White House. In front of the White House, Hechler's company halted, stacking arms in the shade of the fine large trees on the south side of Pennsylvania Avenue. A small crowd of onlookers gathered to gaze at this battle-hardened regiment of volunteers. Soon the command of "Break-ranks!" caused a wild and pell-mell scattering of the men, who vanished quickly to enjoy the worldly pleasures of Washington-some had gastronomical preferences, some female, some just to escape the military routine and gaze at monuments.

INSIDE THE WHITE HOUSE, President Lincoln was receiving two governors, Dennison of Ohio and Pierpont of West Virginia. Soon Lincoln and the two governors came out to view the regiment, and the bugles sounded "Assembly" for the men of Hechler's regiment.

As if by magic, from all directions, the men of the 36th Ohio Volunteer Infantry came running into the rally point. Two infantrymen from Hechler's company, Joe Schofield and Lewis Starbuck, ran up bearing a huge watermelon, with a policeman hot on their heels. The cop shouted an imperious demand for the watermelon, and just as Schofield and Starbuck took their places in ranks in front of the White House and the men stood silently and stiffly at attention, the cop again bellowed loudly for the melon. By now President Lincoln and the two governors were out by the iron fence of the White House, and could not help but observe this unrehearsed scene.

SUDDENLY, THE WATERMELON FELL and burst into red and juicy fragments on Pennsylvania Avenue, just as the officer of the law was closing in with another demand. Without uttering a sound, the boys pointed to the ground with an invitation to the policeman to "Take It." Lincoln and his distinguished guests laughed very heartily as they stood with their shoulders against the iron fence of the White House grounds.

The incident was quickly forgotten as this finely trained regiment put on a swift and snappy exhibition of the manual of arms, then right faced, and by columns of fours marched off down Pennsylvania Avenue to 7th Street, and thence on the road toward Baltimore.

The regiment was bound for Maryland with the rest of the Kanawha Division with the mission trying to repel General Robert E. Lee's invasion of Maryland. At midnight on Sept 8, the regiment camped near Brookville, Maryland. The next day the men were pleased to draw half a day's supply of light bread. Their progress toward Frederick was described by Pvt. George Hechler in a letter to his sister Kate in Marietta:

> We came to Ridgeville by easy marches, where we heard that several hundred recruits for the Rebel Army had passed the night before, and our cavalry drove in Rebel pickets on the way toward Frederick City.
>
> The next morning we started and went through New Market about 11 o'clock. Nearly all the inhabitants are Secesh of the bitterest kind. Our division now took the advance to Frederick, where we stopped for the night after routing the rear guard of the Rebels. Next day we went to Middletown, our advance skirmishing all the way. On the hill between both towns, overlooking the country around, we stopped and rested a little while, and many remarked that this country is worth fighting for. It is the most beautiful we have yet seen in our travels. At the highest levels of command, far above the concern of a mere private and combat infantryman, again there was swirling discontent. General Pope's defeat at the Second Battle of Bull Run prompted an outcry for McClellan's return. The proud and vain McClellan, who had always over-estimated the size of Lee's forces by about 100 per cent

> and then used these estimates as his explanation for his over cautiousness, was nevertheless respected as an organizer. Against his better judgment, Lincoln gave McClellan another chance, since Pope's failure at Second Bull Run was so shattering.

Along with 35,000 men under the somewhat soiled banner of General McClellan, brothers John and George Hechler marched into Maryland, bound for South Mountain and then for a town whose name in Civil War annals is synonymous with blood and carnage: Antietam.

21. Union Forces Get Tumultuous Welcome

Frederick, Maryland Is Liberated — Different Story Free and Liberators — Secure Top Secret Order

BARBARA FRIETCHIE, who was immortalized by John Greenleaf Whittier's poem, was the legendary woman of courage who held aloft the stars and stripes which the Rebels tried to shoot down in the town of Frederick, Maryland.

Pvt. Hechler in later years enjoyed Whittier's moving and patriotic account, but when Hechler marched into Frederick in September, 1862, neither he nor anyone else saw or heard anyone tell of Dame Barbara Frietchie. In any event, nobody before or since has described the weather or scenery of Frederick better than Whittier's opening lines:

> Up from the meadows rich with corn
> Clear in the cool September morn
> The clustered spires of Frederick stand
> Green-walled by the hills of Maryland
> Round about them orchards sweep
> Apple and peach tree fruited deep
> Fair as the garden of the Lord
> To the eyes of the famished Rebel horde.

Going into the town of New Market, Maryland, Hechler's company passed through a covered bridge over a stream called the Conecocheague. As one of the boys put it, the name was almost as long as the stream was wide. Hurrying onward, they surprised a detachment of Rebel cavalry so suddenly that they rode away before the horses could eat any of the corn which had been thrown on the ground for them.

BUT THE STORY was a little different in the town of Frederick. General Lee's army was in possession of the town on September 12, 1862 as the Union troops approached. The Hechler brothers were in the Kanawha Division, which moved forward as the advance force of the army. Several Rebel artillery pieces were placed on the outskirts of the town, but as the Union forces approached Frederick the Rebel guns were withdrawn into town.

Now Hechler's brigade commander, Col. Moore, joined a group of cavalry which recklessly charged the town. As described by Captain Jewett Palmer, Hechler's company commander:

> Away went our fellows down the principal street yelling like Indians. Soon a brisk volley came up from the center of town and in a little while our fellows came out closely pursued by the Rebels. Col. Moore, who had rashly followed our cavalry, was taken prisoner and two of his staff wounded. General Crook then took command of our brigade and soon drove the enemy out of the city. Our loss was one killed and six wounded, and the Rebel loss six killed. About 50 of their sick fell into our hands. As we passed through the place the stars and stripes were displayed at almost every house and the ladies welcomed us with demonstrations of joy. They were delivered from the hands of the Philistines.

IN FACT, THE ENTRANCE INTO FREDERICK was one of the most tumultuous which Hechler experienced during the entire war. Along the National Pike, the main thoroughfare through Frederick, windows, balconies, porch-roofs, house-tops—every available spot facing the main street was pre-empted by happy people greeting their liberators. Fluttering and waving in the breeze were flags of all sizes and descriptions Hot tea and coffee, sandwiches, milk, and even pie and cake was eagerly handed to the passing troops.

General McClellan, who resembled General MacArthur in his showmanship, proudly rode his flashing steed, "Devil Dan," to capture the greatest crescendo of cheers. Young women thronged around Devil Dan and soon had him fully decorated with red, white and blue ribbons. His mane and even his tail were fully covered with flags and other decorations. General McClellan gladly submitted to more flags in his saddle, stirrups and boot-tops. Writing to his wife, General McClellan said: "Why, even Dan caught the spirit of the occasion and as regally accepted the attention as if the entire affair were in his honor."

Once the parade and festivities were over, it was back to work for Pvt. Hechler and his buddies. A little after noon on September 13, the men of the 36th Ohio Volunteer Infantry resumed their march out the National Pike from Frederick. They headed into the fabulously rich and picturesque Catoctin Valley. The sergeant major of Hechler's company John T. Booth, waxed lyrical when describing the scene in his diary. "At this season of the year," Sgt. Booth wrote, "Nature, clad in her rich autumnal robes, presents, in this region, unusual attractions. As we reached the summit of the Catoctin range on this afternoon's march, there suddenly burst upon our enraptured view a kaleidoscopic panorama of pastoral beauty and grandeur that is seldom given to mortal eye to look upon."

SUDDENLY THERE OCCURRED one of the fateful events of war which furnish the opportunity for one side or the other to seize the initiative in a decisive fashion. Had McClellan been a man of action and decision, he might have dealt a back-breaking blow to Lee's army. For late on the 13th of September, there fell into Union hands a copy of a top secret order detailing Lee's plans and intentions, as well as the disposition of his forces. McClellan knew now that Stonewall Jackson and his corps were over at Harpers Ferry trying to reduce that post. And he knew that many miles separated Jackson from the bulk of Lee's forces. Even in the certain knowledge of these factors, McClellan dawdled and continued business as usual.

This was a major factor in McClellan's failure to deal a decisive blow for the Union forces in the battles of South Mountain and Antietam. The failure to win what could have been a major victory was a bitter pill for the men to swallow. For others, South Mountain and Antietam meant crippling wounds or death itself. For Pvt. George Hechler, Antietam meant a confused and tangled nightmare of war, and the first and only wound he received during the hostilities.

22. Marietta Company in Bayonet Charge

Battle of South Mountain — Rebels Pushed Back
Captain Palmer — Proud of Division — Reinforcements

FROM WEST VIRGINIA'S eastern panhandle you can throw a rock and hit the bloody battlefield of Antietam.

Between Frederick, Maryland, and Antietam, South Mountain lay athwart the path of the Union armies of Genearl McClellan. Proud and pompous, McClellan had superiority in numbers, but he was cleverly out-generaled by Robert E. Lee and his gray and butternut battalions.

A native West Virginian named Stonewall Jackson in mid-September of 1862 smashed at the Union garrison in Harpers Ferry, trapped them, and took 11,000 prisoners. Now McClellan threw his forces, including Hechler's regiment, into action in the Battle of South Mountain.

The regiment moved out toward South Mountain on Sunday morning, skirmishers ahead Hechler piled his knapsack on the ground where he had slept the night before. The invalids stayed behind at the bivouac, guarding the knapsacks. "Forward!" cried the company commanders, as the column marched through newly-sown wheat fields, and orchards laden with apples. Cannonading signaled the presence of the Rebels on South Mountain as Hechler and his fellow infantrymen cautiously advanced to the base of the mountain.

THE REBELS were gradually pushed back by Union troops in advance of Hechler's regiment, and after a fierce fire fight the Rebels

General James Longstreet

drew up their forces just over the brow of the mountain. Now two brigades of Union infantrymen, including the 36th Ohio Volunteer Infantry, were thrown into line facing the summit of the mountain. As soon as this was done, the men were ordered to lie down. According to young Jewett Palmer, Hechler's company commander: "After that, it was as much as a man's life was worth to stand up, for the enemy were not 15 paces from us, just over the summit."

It was about nine o'clock in the morning, sunny and clear, with every element of the landscape etched sharply. A strange silence descended on the battlefield. Both armies waited for the other to make the first move.

Suddenly Pvt. Hechler observed his brigade commander, General George Crook riding below on his horse "Charlie." Col. Crook, the taciturn Indian fighter, gave his command quickly and directly: "Boys, give them the cold steel. Fix bayonets! Forward, double-quick, Charge!!"

THE YOUNG MARIETTA company commander of Hechler's Company G, Capt. Jewett Palmer, wrote in his diary: "Hardly had the command been given when my regiment moved up in one of the handsomest lines I ever saw." Hechler's company, bayonets flashing in the sun, advanced in front of the regiment and began firing on the Rebels. General Crook, throwing his hat aloft with one hand and holding his sword on high with the other, shouted: "36th, Charge!!" The line in blue surged forward with terrible yells. The Rebels were routed, but reformed and counter-attacked. Several counterattacks were repulsed.

Supporting the Hechler's regiment in the bayonet charge was the regiment commanded by a lieutenant colonel who was later to become President of the United States: Rutherford B. Hayes. The commander of the Kanawha Division, Maj. Gen. Jacob D. Cox, described the action in a few well-chosen words: "Crook's column had come into close support. Bayonets were fixed, and at the word the line rushed forward with loud hurrahs. Hayes, being in the woods, was not seen till he had passed over the crest and turned upon the enemy's flank and rear. Here was a sharp combat, but our men established themselves upon the summit and drove the enemy before them."

GENERAL COX was proud of his division's performance at South Mountain. He wrote in his reminiscences:

> In our mountain camps of West Virginia, I had felt discontented that our native Ohio regiments did not take as kindly to the labors of drill and camp police as some of German birth, and I had warned them that they would feel the need of accuracy and mechanical precision when the day of battle came. They had done reasonably well, but suffered in comparison with some of the others on dress parade and in the form and neatness of the camp. When, however, in the slopes of South Mountain I saw the

> lines go forward steadier and more even under fire than they had ever done at drill, their intelligence making them perfectly comprehend the advantage of unity in their effort and in the shock when they met the foe, when their bodies seemed to dilate, their step to have better cadence and a tread as of giants as they went cheering up the hill, I took back all my criticisms and felt a pride and glory in them as soldiers and comrades that words cannot express.

HOLDING THE CREST of South Mountain, Hechler's regiment anxiously awaited reinforcements. Southern prisoners caused some apprehension when they relayed the information that Confederate Generals Longstreet and Hill were both in front of the Kanawha Division with their entire commands. There was only one small, tired and bloodied Union division hanging on to the crest of South Mountain in the face of this giant force. But at length a cloud of dust told Hechler's men that succor was at hand. Yet the reinforcements did not arrive until the enemy had made several charges in an attempt to recapture the crest.

In a letter to his sister Kate in Marietta, Pvt. Hechler described the battle matter-of-factly:

> Sunday morning, about daylight, started again, and soon found the Rebels in force, but drove them back to the top of South Mountain without much loss, but there they seemed determined to stop our further advance. In less than half an hour after we formed in line, the front of our Regiment was cleared of Rebels. We fell back a few rods and lay down, and soon the Rebel artillery commenced a furious cannonading for several hours, but only wounded a few. Our artillery slowly replied. By this time, the Rebels received reinforcements and were forming again on the other side of the hill behind stone walls, but our columns could be seen coming in the distance. We anxiously waited about two hours when the rattle of muskets on our right told us that

> the battle had commenced again. Our regiment moved toward that place but was held in reserve that evening.

That night, Hechler and his fellow infantrymen slept on their arms on the battlefield. The next morning dawned on a fearful sight. Many a brave southerner lay stiff and cold among the tangled and bloody laurel.

This was the prelude to Antietam.

23. Pvt. Hechler Wounded During Shelling

Ohio Regiment in Potomac Campaign
Shells Drop Close — Firing Dies Down

In the crisp fresh mountain air of Western Maryland, the great and gallant Robert E. Lee massed his meager columns in September of 1862. Lee invaded Maryland as a prelude to moving into Pennsylvania and to bring the war to the Union's front doorstep.

With twice as many men in blue, General McClellan could afford to say overconfidently: "My general idea is to cut the enemy in two and beat him in detail." At the Battle of South Mountain, fought on September 14, 1862, a spirited bayonet charge by the 36th Ohio Volunteer Infantry Regiment (Pvt. Hechler's regiment) helped carry the day. But a West Virginia major general and corps commander, Jesse L. Reno, lay dead on the South Mountain battlefield.

At the White House, President Abraham Lincoln telegraphed General McClellan after South Mountain: "God bless you and all with you. Destroy the Rebel army, if possible." With 87,000 men, the overcautious McClellan moved westward to engage Lee's ragged 30,000 along a sluggish creek named the Antietam in one of the bloodiest battles of the war.

For Pvt. George Hechler, September 15, 1862 dawned fresh and very chilly. He had slept on the South Mountain battlefield, shivering until after midnight when blankets were brought up. After sunrise, he was appalled to see the results of the battle. One of Hechler's company officers Lt. W. S. Stanley, wrote in his diary: "In one place not 20 feet square I counted 16 dead Rebels. They lie scattered all through

Lt. Wallace S. Stanley

the woods, thickets and open fields. Many are so hid away among the laurel that they will not be found and their bones in after years will startle the visitor to the battlefield."

Then Hechler's regiment fell in and started down the mountain, and there soon burst into view a panorama which caused the men to linger and drink in the beauty. Sgt. John T. Booth described it in this way: "In the distance-in a visual sweep of some eight to twelve miles in front, rolls lazily, along on its tortuous bed, the dark current of the Potomac. On this side of the Potomac, some six to eight miles from the mountain pass through which we are descending, runs the drowsy stream called the Antietam Creek, flowing almost due south, falling into the Potomac about eight miles above Harpers Ferry, forming with the river, as we view it, a sort of an irregular acute angle."

Hechler's regiment marched about five miles, and bivouacked in a ploughed field. The next day, September 16, Hechler witnessed one of the grandest artillery duels he had ever seen or heard. About 150 cannon were engaged. The regiment was bivouacked on the flank near some timber, and from their position the artillery duel was distinctly visible. Finally the Rebels withdrew their guns. Shortly after this, the entire Kanawha Division of which Hechler's regiment was an important part was ordered to take up a more advanced position near a bridge crossing Antietam Creek.

THE 36TH REGIMENT moved out in division advance, through a sunken cornfield, and before long became warmly engaged with the skirmishers of the main body of the Rebel army. Then the shells started dropping in uncomfortably close. General Crook ordered his men to lie down and shelter themselves as much as possible. Lt. Stanley, one of Hechler's company officers, reported: "I was lying down with my sword across my breast when a piece of shell struck it fair and square, but did no injury."

Pvt. Hechler was not quite as lucky. He was wounded by a shell, but knowing that his sister and his family would be worried by the news, he tried to make light of it in his letter to his sister Kate in Marietta.

> There was considerable artillery firing in the forenoon. After noon, we were ordered to the left wing where the Rebels commenced shelling us, but did little damage beyond scaring a few pretty badly, who returned to the rear. Their pieces of shell came close. One of them struck my foot but did not cut the shoe, and the next day the swelling had gone down low enough so I could wear my shoe again and keep up with the company.

BY 9 O'CLOCK on the evening of September 16, shot and shell gradually began to die down. Lt. Col . Melvin Clarke, a leading member of the Marietta bar who had risen to the command of the 36th Ohio Volunteer Infantry Regiment, counseled with his troops and advised the men to make themselves as comfortable as possible for the night. He authorized one man from each company mess to go out in search of water. Col. Clarke's solicitude for his men made them love and respect him, and made his regiment above average because the men, well-trained by Gen. Crook, would follow Col. Clarke because they had confidence in his leadership.

On the eve of the sharpest action at Antietam, Pvt. Hechler lay painfully wounded on the battlefield. Yet his wound was not serious enough to warrant more than a perfunctory visit to the aid station. For the popular regimental commander, Col. Clarke, the sands in the hour-glass of life were running out. On September 17, the 36th Ohio Volunteer Infantry Regiment was to lose the first of a series of commanding officers, mortally wounded in combat.

One of the top historians of the Civil War had some well-chosen words for the battle-scarred regiment of which Pvt. Hechler was a member. "There was a subtle difference between them and the rest of the army," wrote Bruce Catton. "They were more informal in bearing and discipline, and it was noticed that they marched with a longer, freer stride: the army of the Potomac had been rigorously drilled to the regulation pace of twenty-eight inches, while the Westerners had been allowed to set their own gait."

Thus it was on the evening of September 16 as a proud regiment slept on its arms on the banks of Antietam Creek: a Marietta farm boy with a puffed up and painfully throbbing foot; a lawyer from Marietta who had less than 24 hours to live; and less than a hundred miles away in the White House, a President who was praying for a victory.

24. A Son of Marietta Is Killed

Col. Clarke Killed at Antietam — Bitter Disappointment Could See Lee's Forces

In mid-September of 1862, Abraham Lincoln sorely needed a victory. The President kept his ear glued to the telegraph key, praying that it would spell out that the Union forces in blue had triumphed over the Confederates at Antietam.

Water was scarce in Pvt. Hechler's company, not because it was not available, but because the boys were not allowed to get out into the open area where shells were dropping in at a fast rate. On the morning of September 17, just as the regimental mail arrived a shell burst in the middle of several stacks of guns and threw the guns to the ground. With equal speed, the mailman emptied his mail on the ground. As the carrier speedily vamoosed, Hechler and his buddies looked hungrily at the bushel or more of letters from home which they did not dare to go out and touch as long as the heavy shelling persisted.

The commander of Hechler's brigade, Indian fighter Brig. Gen. George Crook, had his troops on the far right. They were part of the corps troops of General Ambrose Burnside, an amiable commander whose chief distinction was the whiskers by which his name became a household word. The mercurial General McClellan had this to say in his report on Antietam: "Early in the morning of the 17th, I ordered General Burnside to form his troops and hold them in readiness to assault the bridge in his front and await further orders. Crook's brigade was ordered to storm the bridge." The bridge, a stone structure with three arches and stone parapets, was commanded by steep banks on the opposite side and the Confederates had the bridge approaches heavily defended. This strategic structure became known as the "Burnside Bridge."

AS IT TURNED OUT, Hechler's brigade drew up to the bridge but before they made an assault crossing several batteries of artillery were summoned to pound the opposite banks. In the confusion another unit made the first crossing, which was a bitter disappointment to General Crook. Just across the Burnside Bridge, Hechler's 36th Regiment was ordered to attack in the face of withering enemy fire. The attack was made over rolling and ascending ground that had been ploughed and was very rough, and over rail and stone fences heavily guarded. In the words of Sgt. John T. Booth of Hechler's company, "While we were crossing these fences the enemy's sharpshooters gave us their strenuous and unremitting attention."

In a letter to his sister Kate in Marietta, Pvt. Hechler describes the Battle of Antietam, and how his own regimental commander, Lt. Col. Melvin Clarke, was killed in front of his eyes. Here is what Pvt. Hechler wrote about Antietam:

> We were not engaged in the forenoon, and in the afternoon when ordered forward we were greeted with a perfect storm of grape and canister which killed and wounded a few, but cut many more. We lost sacks and blankets-some lost theirs by the strap being cut-among them was mine. After going about fifty yards further we had reached a low point where we could not be seen by the Rebels. Here Colonel Clarke said 'Get your places and lie down.' These were the last words he spoke for he had scarcely finished them when a cannon ball whistled over our heads and struck him. He was a few steps behind the line but he did not speak a word. Afterwards, his expression when, as he cast his eyes along the Regiment, was 'Oh oh, oh!' and he fainted away and died about five minutes afterward.

The 36th Ohio Volunteer Infantry Regiment was greatly shocked by Col. Clarke's death, for he was deeply respected, honored and loved by his men. Col. Clarke was one of the original founders of the 36th Ohio Volunteer Infantry Regiment, being the recipient of a telegram from Congressman William P. Cutler on July 23, 1861, asking him to raise and organize the regiment.

Not more than a few minutes after Col. Clarke fell mortally wounded, the brigade commander General Crook came along, cast a sad look at his late friend and companion in arms, and then took personal charge of the regiment.

Continuing his description of the Battle of Antietam, after writing of the death of his regimental commander, Pvt. Hechler wrote to his sister:

> But soon our line began to give way right and left, the enemy pressing them. We rallied again, but could not drive the Rebels, so we were again ordered to fall back and formed another line on the ground the Rebels had in the morning. This was all the advantage we had. Some of our regiments could not number fifty men. Many of their bravest lay dead or wounded on a field in possession of the enemy and we lay down in line, expecting a fight that night. All passed off quietly, and in the morning skirmishing commenced early but nothing was done all day.

THAT NIGHT PVT. HECHLER and the rest of the men of the regiment were bivouacked near a fence. When the moon came up, Hechler could see Lee's forces retreating along the road which leads from Sharpsburg to the Potomac. The road leads along a sort of "hogback" or ridge, and the Confederate forces could easily be seen silhouetted against the moonlit sky.

Pvt. Hechler was thankful, as he lay on the battlefield of Antietam, that he had escaped with nothing more serious than a foot wound in the battle. He reflected on the brave men who had fallen that day, with the realization that shot and shell know no distinctions of rank as they mow down privates, generals and beloved regimental commanders like Lt. Col. Melvin Clarke.

In the White House, President Lincoln took stock of the news from the Antietam Battlefield. It was not a complete victory. Once again the cautious McClellan had been out-generalled by Robert E. Lee, and Lee's main army was allowed to escape. Yet the outcome was optimistic enough to prompt Abraham Lincoln to take the boldest step of the war and decide to go ahead with issuance of the Emancipation Proclamation.

25. Thirty-sixth Infantry at Antietam

1.2 Million Rebels

In 1902 the Ohio Antietam Battlefield Commission published a hardcover book which reflected a retrospective account not only of what had occurred at Antietam—the bloodiest battle of the Civil War—but also related a fuller history of George Hechler's regiment, the 36th Ohio Volunteer Infantry. Excerpts from the 1902 commission report follow:

After the Battle of Bull Run (first), while excitement ran high in Washington City, President Lincoln authorized Hon. William Cutler, M.C., to have a regiment recruited at Marietta, Ohio. As result, the 36th Ohio.

Camp Putnam, adjoining the city, was its rendezvous. By August 17, 1861, ten companies of volunteers had assembled there, and by August 27 organization was completed, and they were mustered in by Henry Belknap, Captain 18th United States Infantry.

On the 31st six companies marched into West Virginia for the purpose of breaking up predatory bands of bushwhackers. The first day out the regiment sustained its first loss in the accidental death of young Steward, of Company A.

That portion of the regiment remaining at Parkersburg was under command of Lieutenant-Colonel Clarke. October 5th it embarked on the Ben Franklin, landing at Camp Piatt, head of navigation on the Big Kanawha, Sunday, October 6th. October 19th Lieutenant-Colonel Clarke's command started for Summersville, where it arrived P.M., October 22nd.

The winter of 1861-2 was a very trying one upon the regiment. Typhus and other camp diseases prevailed. Deaths were frequent. As many as three were laid away in a day, some fifty in all that winter.

General Fremont being called off from his march on Lynchburg, Virginia, to attack Stonewall Jackson, General J. D. Cox, of whose command the 3d Provisional was a part, was informed that the concerted movement he was to make with Fremont was abandoned, therefore he must use his own discretion in protecting his command against the Rebel forces in his proximity, which were now left free to concentrate upon him. The enemy assuming the aggressive, Cox, with his immediate command, May 21st, retired to a defensible position on Flat Top Mountain. This left Crook far to the front and unsupported. May 29, Crook also retired fifteen miles and established his brigade in the strong defensible position at Meadow's Bluff. From this point he essayed two extended raids far into the enemy's territory, the enemy retiring. General Cox, commanding the Kanawha Division, was ordered to join Pope in the East. August 15th the 36th filed out of camp, headed for Camp Piatt, ninety miles distant, where it arrived P.M. 17th. A.M. 18th the division embarked, the 36th on the *Allen Collier*, *General Meigs* and *Pike*, for Parkersburg. Arrived at their former camp on the 29th, and found a camp full of relatives and recruits, awaiting. P.M. of 25th, boarded palatial (?) hog car for Pope's army, passing through Washington, D. C., was hurried across the Potomac, arriving at Warrenton Junction, 24th; disembarking after a sixty hour ride. The sound of battle was there and continued sounding in our ears until our return to Arlington. On evening of the 25th, the regiment held dress parade. There were among the onlookers many generals, among others Pope, who was so pleased as to pay the regiment a high compliment. A raid of the enemy had divided the Kanawha, so that but part of the brigade reached the front. Possibly, partially at least, owing to this fact the 36th was assigned at Pope's headquarters as guard, and as such were held as reserves.

At 7 A.M., September 6th, the regiment left Arlington, marched through Jordansville, across the old aqueduct, through Georgetown, and up Pennsylvania Avenue to front of White House, there halted and stacked arms.

The regiment marched out Seventh street to the old Scott camp ground and bivouacked.

The Maryland campaign was on.

The Kanawha Division was assigned to the 9th Corps, Reno commanding. McClellan's report says: "The right wing, consisting of 1st and 9th Corps, under command of Major-General Burnside, moved on Frederick City, the 9th Corps via New Market, Reno and Seventh Street Road." General Strother (Port Crayon), formerly of Pope's, now of McClellan's staff, says: "We have news that the enemy has crossed the Potomac, and his advance, 5,000 strong, marched in to Frederick City this morning. This afternoon a column of 20,000 infantry, with 60 pieces of cannon, moved up street leading toward Frederick. Events are progressing so rapidly that we have no time for speculation. Lee is actually across the Potomac. It must be their necessity, and not their hopes, which urges them to their desperate venture."

September 7th, the head of column began that long to be remembered "Sabbath day's journey." Heat, dust, thirst, intense, stifling. Men by the hundreds fell by the wayside, many dying. About 4 P.M. went into bivouac near Leesboro,on a slight elevation in a meadow, the most beautiful spot ever occupied by the roadway, as it wound up the hill, were covered with rifle-pits and breastworks of rails, etc. These works and the woods that covered the slopes were filled with the enemy's riflemen, and batteries were in position to enfilade the bridge and its approaches. From Colonel Crook's position it was found impossible to carry the bridge. Colonel Crook brought a section of Simmons' Battery to a position to command the bridge. The 51st New York and the 51st Pennsylvania were then ordered to assault the bridge. The reports of Generals Burnside, Cox and other division commanders, are in line with above quotation and will be referred to further along.

Early in the morning heavy cannonading was heard far on our right, telling us the battle was on in earnest. Shortly after these sounds broke in upon us, several shells came hurtling into our camp in the sunken cornfield, one of them knocking down several stacks of guns. Immediately thereafter the regiment marched toward the front. Notwithstanding severe fighting had been indulged in, in an effort to take number 3 (Burnside) bridge, the 36th did not until later become actively engaged-not, indeed, until after it had crossed the bridge; this it did without firing a gun. After crossing, it formed below the bridge under the low hill bordering the stream, its right extending nearly to the Sharpsburg Road. Here it remained well sheltered, until probably about 3 P.M., when it was ordered to advance. This movement was made on the double-quick over rolling and ascending ground that had been ploughed and was very rough, and over post and rail fences, so staunch they had to be climbed. While we were crossing these fences the enemy's sharpshooters gave us their strenuous and unremitting attention. While crossing the two small ridges it was under heavy fire of grape and canister; the enemy's guns were posted on a knoll that afforded them full sway of the ground the regiment was compelled to pass over. Just as the regiment had passed over the second roll of ground into a shallow swale, Colonel Clarke gave the command to "lie down"—"Men, lie down, every one of you." He motioned his command with his sword. As he uttered the command a shot from a Rebel gun on our left front, where the enemy was heavily massed, struck him on the right thigh at its junction with the hip. He fell, dying in a few seconds. The regiment was greatly shocked thereby, for he was deeply respected, honored and loved by his men. Ten days before he had been promoted to succeed Crook to the colonelcy of the regiment, but, I believe, had not learned of his newly acquired honor. After resting in that hollow for a short time, the regiment moved forward to a stone fence near the summit of the hill immediately overlooking Sharpsburg. Here it halted and engaged the enemy, witnessing also the heavy fighting on either wing. Said Sergeant True of G: "It was while we lay behind this fence that the battle on the left was lost. A few more troops put in promptly on our left and pushed forward would have gained us a very decided victory. From where we lay by that fence, we could see enough men behind Antietam not at all in action, to have rolled up Lee's right like a scroll."

From the viewpoint occupied by the regiment like opinion, as expressed by Sergeant M. C. True, impressed itself upon the thinking men of the regiment. Darkness was growing apace, the drawing of night's curtain was gradually shutting out the scenes. Our forces to our right and left not having advanced so far as the 36th and those with it, we were left without adequate support on either flank. The regiment was withdrawn, and under the shades of evening repaired to its former position near the bridge on the brow of the hill overlooking the bridge and creek and slept on arms all night.

The battle of Antietam had passed into history.

The regiment's casualties were 3 killed, 21 wounded and 2 missing.

How the 36th missed the glory of being the first regiment to cross Burnside bridge, and Colonel Crook disappointed!

If my readers will read the reports of McClellan Burnside, Cox, Crook, et al., of Antietam, they will comprehend the disappointment that befell the Colonel and his regiment.

When regimental historian John T. Booth was compiling history, he edited this response from Gen. Crook:

HEADQUARTERS DEPARTMENT OF THE PLATTE,
OMAHA, NEBRASKA, December 19, 1887

John T. Booth, M.C.:

My Dear Doctor: —Yours 12th instant, just as hand. On the morning of the 17th of September, Captain Christie, of General Cox's staff, came to me while we were lying in that sunken cornfield, where, you remember, we passed the night, and told me that General Sturgis Division has failed to take the bridge, or had been repulsed, I don't just recall the language now; upon my inquiring where the bridge was, he replied, 'Damned if I know,' but supposed it was in the direction he pointed. Upon my remonstrating against such an indefinite order he replied in a curt manner that he had done his duty in giving the order and it was my duty to obey it. Having heard the firing in the morning in the direction pointed out by Chrisitem, I went forward with the 11th Ohio to reconnoiter. We had not proceeded far before we came across the dead and wounded of General Sturgis Division. I went sufficiently far in advance to see the situation and to convince myself that the bridge could not be taken from that point. I left the 11th Ohio where it was and took the 28th Ohio and a section of Simmonds Battery to the right of the 11th and up the creek into some small hills, leaving the 36th in the road near the brick house. I posted the section of artillery on a point that enfiladed the enemy's position and, in the meantime, had directed part of the 28th to cross the creek above the bridge by wading the stream, keeping the remainder of the 28th as a support to the artillery. My intention was to cross the bridge with the 36th Ohio myself. In a short time after opening of the battery's fire and the crossing of the 28th above the position of the enemy, they retreated, and by that time I reached the 36th, two regiments of some other command walked across the bridge without having anything to do with taking it. I may also add that these two regiments referred to were the first troops I saw outside of our own command. If any other troops than our brigade had anything to do with the taking of the bridge, I don't know it. I feel sure in my own mind they didn't have.

Yours sincerely,
George Crook.

The quiet after the storm was almost frightening in its contrast. On the night of September 23, 1862, reveille was sounded at 3 a.m. owing to a rumored attack. Sixty rounds of cartridges were issued to every man in Hechler's company. After being alerted and on edge, the men waited and waited and waited. The wagons were loaded, but still nothing happened. And no move was ordered.

As the first chill of fall stimulated a greater number of campfires, so did the "grapevine" rumors grow. First it was that Hechler's company would follow the "Johnnie Rebs" down through the Shenandoah Valley. But most of the boys wanted to get back to West Virginia. The Rebels had driven the Union forces and most of the active sympathizers out of the Kanawha Valley, and there was a great anxiety for the safety of people in this important area.

SOON THE WAITING became almost intolerable, both for the men and for the Commander in Chief in the White House, General McCellan sent repeated calls for more shoes, mules and horses. To one of these pleas, President Lincoln replied: "I have just read your dispatch about sore-tongued and fatigued horses. Will you pardon me for asking what the horses of your army have done since the battle of Antietam that fatigues anything?"

Early in October, while General McClellan was resting his troops of the Army of the Potomac, a visitor at the White House asked Lincoln how many men the Confederates had in the field. Seriously, the President answered: "1,200,000 according to the best authority." The visitor turned pale and cried: "My God, it couldn't be that many!" But the President went on: "Yes, sir, 1,200,000-no doubt of it. You see, all our generals, when they get whipped, say the enemy outnumbers them three to one, and I must believe them. We have 400,000 men in the field, and three times that many makes 1,200,000. Don't you see it?"

Finally, Lincoln resolved to go out and see for himself. He visited the Army of the Potomac in the field. For Pvt. Hechler and his company, this was a red-letter occasion. Lincoln wondered as the vain McClellan kept referring to the boys as "My army."

It was still very dimly gray before dawn as the President rose from his rude cot in his assigned tent out in the field. He shook an Illinois friend named O. M. Hatch and said: "Come, Hatch, I want you to walk with me." Without a word, Hatch got up, the two men dressed and left the tent quietly. The tall, sad-eyed President led Hatch through rows and rows of a great tented city where Pvt. Hechler and thousands of men were sleeping. Hatch noted later: "Lincoln seemed to be peculiarly serious, and his quiet abstracted way affected me also. It did not seem a time to speak." They reached a commanding point in the hills where they could catch a glimpse of the first glow-of the rising sun.

The President waved his hand in a gesture of half-despair, and leaning toward Hatch, said in a husky and almost whispering voice, "Hatch—Hatch, what is all this?"

"Why, Mr. Lincoln," said Hatch, "this is the Army of the Potomac."

Lincoln hesitated a moment, and then straightening up, in a louder and clearer tone of voice, "No, Hatch, no. This is General McClellan's bodyguard." Nothing more was said. The two men walked slowly back to their tent.

It was October 8 before McClellan's army started to move. Pvt. Hechler wrote to his sister Kate in Marietta:

> On the morning of the 8th of October, we started for Hagerstown and reached the city a little before sundown. We stopped in some fields for the night, and started early next morning to a clearing which we reached at noon, and stopped for the night near a large spring which runs a stream of clear water, the best we had had for some time. At two o'clock the next morning we started for Hancock, 15 miles distant where we forded the Potomac. It was scarcely knee-deep. We stopped at the B & O Railroad, got onto the cars the next night but stopped for two more days before moving. Then we started for Clarksburg, where it was understood we were to be paid and clothed, as many of our clothes were in rags. Our paymaster has come at last, and we are just being paid off as I write this, for six months.
>
> Captain Palmer came into camp day before yesterday and will probably return to Marietta tomorrow, when I shall try and send this letter and some money with him, unless I get a better chance. I shall put 52 dollars in this letter, 50 for safe keeping, and the rest you may send me a few postage stamps and a pair of good wool socks if you get a chance.
>
> Your affectionate brother, George

26. Lincoln Master of Military Strategy

No Railroad for Men in Grey — Rain and Sleet
Union Regiment Moved Back — Telegraph Lines Destroyed
Men Wanted to Halt

THERE IS Greek proverb which reads: "Better an army of deer with a lion for leader, than an army of lions with a deer for leader."

Relating this proverb to the Civil War, there is no question but that the Confederate forces had a lion in Robert E. Lee, and the Union's General George B. McClellan proved to be a deer.

Time and again, President Lincoln urged General McClellan after the Battle of Antietam to move. He advised, exhorted, needled and tried to spur McClellan, sending him detailed instructions, maps, orders, suggestions-all to no avail. The record of this trying period marks Lincoln as a far greater master of military strategy than his professionally trained generals.

The aftermath of Antietam had deep implication for the state of West Virginia. The departure of many Union troops—including Pvt. Hechler's 36th Ohio Regiment-from the Kanawha Valley laid that area open to a series of daring raids by Confederate cavalrymen like General Albert Gallatin Jenkins, who swept through Weston, Buckhannon, Spencer, Ripley and Ravenswood and even crossed the river into Ohio. Now that Lee's retreat freed the Union forces at Antietam, there was tremendous pressure to rescue West Virginia. Therefore, General Jacob D. Cox was ordered to take his Kanawha Division back into the Kanawha Valley and clear out the Confederates.

THEN MEN IN GREY were occupying Virginia so strongly that the B & O Railroad was denied to the Union between Harpers Ferry and Hancock. But by marching overland through Hagerstown to Hancock, the Union forces could use the railroad going westward toward Parkersburg. This they did, sending Pvt. Hechler's regiment as far as Clarksburg and sending additional troops from Parkersburg toward the Kanawha Valley.

For Pvt. Hechler, October, 1862, was a wonderful month. Although Antietam meant the loss of some of his dearest friends, and a combat wound himself, it also meant a promotion. Hechler had now been in the Union Army for a year, and of all the developments in the war the promotion to corporal which occurred after Antietam was his proudest. From Clarksburg, Cpl. Hechler wrote on October 23, 1862, to his sister Kate in Marietta:

> My Dear Sister:
>
> I received your letter of the 12th yesterday evening, and the one of the 19th sent by Mr. Barber on the 20th just after I had sealed up the letter I sent the money in. I sent 52 dollars with our Captain. He promised to take it to Mr. Barber where you can get it without much trouble.
>
> We are getting tents now, and the probability is that we will stay here a few days longer. The most of our officers have gone home on furlough. I have sent you a short sketch of the places we have passed since we left Parkersburg. Perhaps it will be of some interest to you.
>
> We have now good times after our hard campaign, and I am well, as I have been for a long time, as cool weather is coming on and the water is getting colder. But it is only the goodness of God that has spared me through all dangers safely. I hope and pray that He may guard and protect me as long as I will have to live here. And if He sees fit to call me from here soon, take me home with Him where there is not strife nor sorrow, but peace and joy forever.
>
> The recruits from the 11th Ohio Volunteer Infantry came here a few days ago, and the regiment makes considerable of

a show again. The 123rd is also here but I have not seen it yet. There are no less than 15,000 troops about here, but some of them have orders to march today. Our regiment will have to drill.

There is a rumor here that we will take up winter quarters soon, but it is not generally believed and it seems most too early if the Government is in earnest about the war.

It is nearly drill time and I shall close this letter. I remain

Your affectionate brother, George

Since leaving West Virginia in August, Hechler's company had been issued no clothing and they were happy to be able to draw new "duds" when they arrived in Clarksburg. Then toward the end of October it was time to move again. All the teams of horses and wagons in and around Clarksburg were pressed into the service of the Union Army and converted into a vast "freight train" to be known as "Crook's train" after the taciturn general who commanded Hechler's brigade.

THE MORNING OF October 27, 1862 dawned amid a cold mixture of rain and sleet. It was extremely difficult to get the mess fires lighted and kept burning. When the bugles sounded "Fall in!" the troops moved hurriedly to strike tents. Then Hechler and his buddies stood for nearly two hours in the sleet and slush, shivering and shaking. It was Army custom, from time immemorial, to hurry up and wait. Finally, the Kanawha Division swung out on the march to Weston and Summersville, with the 36th Ohio and Volunteer Infantry Regiment at the advance of the division, and Hechler's Company G at the advance of the regiment.

It was with mixed feelings that Hechler's company returned to Summersville, where they had trained so rigorously in the winter of 1861. One of Hechler's close friends, Will Stanley, who had just been promoted to 2nd lieutenant in Hechler's company penned a little note home to express his feelings in this fashion:

"Folks at home:

"I once more address you from the land of mountains, laurel and our line of march will be through Weston to Bulltown and along the same pike which the 36th traversed a little more than a year ago and on to Summersville and perhaps to Gauley Bridge. Maybe we will winter in our old quarters. God forbid it, say I, for forty-one of our men already lie beneath the cold, rock sod of Nicholas County and if others must leave us I want it to be on the field of battle."

THE NOTED CINCINNATI Correspondent Whitelaw Reid, author of the two-volume work entitled "Ohio in the War," states "West Virginia was the gift of Ohio, through her State militia, to the Nation at the outset of the War."

What Reid meant was that West Virginia was really saved for the Union cause by Ohio troops. There is a large measure of truth in this assertion.

When Pvt. George Hechler's regiment and other Union troops were moved from West Virginia to fight at Antietam and South Mountain, the Confederates filled the vacuum and began to run wild in the Kanawha Valley. So in October, 1862 thanks to the B & O Railroad, Hechler's regiment was moved back to Clarksburg, and then marched to Summersville in Nicholas County.

As described by Division Commander General George Crook: "Soon after we left the Kanawha Valley, the enemy, under General Loring, drove our people out of that country. So I was ordered back to take possession of that country. Soon after we started, Gen. J. E. B. Stuart of Rebel fame made a raid in the rear of our lines. So I marched from Clarksburg across the country so as to strike the Kanawha Valley high up, and come on the enemy's flank. But as I neared the Valley, they evacuated without any resistance.

ON NOVEMBER 1st, 1862, Hechler's regiment left Sutton at 7 in the morning, and by 1:20 p.m. they crossed the line between Braxton and Nicholas counties. The Rebels had successfully destroyed all the telegraph lines, and a Marietta boy named Joe Ruggles led the Union repair crew in replacing the valuable lines. Much of the country the

CONFEDERATE GENERAL J. E. B. "JEB" STUART

regiment went through was mountainous, almost unbroken wilderness, rough, wild and primitive and sparsely settled. The streams were well stocked with fish and the area abounded with oak, beech, maple, walnut, hickory, poplar, pine, chestnut and cherry trees.

From Summersville, an old familiar area where Hechler had trained when he first joined the regiment, he penned a letter to his sister Kate in Marietta on November 4, 1862:

> My Dear Sister:
>
> I received your letter dated October 24th on the 28th, at Jacksonville, a town of four or five houses about 37 miles from Clarksburg on the road to Summersville.

We are camped now in Summersville, West Virginia. We came here day before yesterday and I should have written you yesterday but I had the rheumatism so bad I could not do anything, and I don't know whether you will be able to read this or not, as my hand is trembling today.

We were welcomed by the citizens around here, who are heartily tired of Rebel rule. There were 400 Rebel cavalry here and the bounty had to keep them, but they left a day or two before we came.

Captain Jewett Palmer, our company commander, has not come back to us yet. I do not know when we will move from here, but I think before many days, as there could not be supplies hauled here for any length of time for as much forces as we have here. Some of the houses have been burned, among them the one which company G occupied last winter.

The way you want to lend the money will suit very well, but do not lend it for longer than one year's time.

Brother John is well yet. It is getting very warm today in the sun, but last night was a very cold night.

We like our regimental officers well enough. Col. Andrews commands a brigade, and Devol the 36th Regiment, but the place of General Crook can never be filled-at least not in the confidence of the men.

I shall have to close this letter, so goodby.

I remain

Your loving brother, GEORGE

On November 11, 1862, with Hechler's company at the head of the regimental column, the Union forces at Summersville marched out at 7 a.m. bound toward Gauley Bridge. The band played old-time tunes as the troops swung out of their old quarters.

General Crook and the members of his staff stood in the doorway of the headquarters reviewing the regiment as the men proudly filed by their old commander. The new regimental commander, Hiram F. Devol of Waterford Township, Ohio, had commanded Company A of the 36th Ohio Volunteer Infantry at the outbreak of the war.

For the third time in the war, Hechler's regiment returned to that fabulous junction of rivers known as Gauley Bridge—the gateway through which all important troop movements from the east into southwestern West Virginia must pass. This was the most advanced post guarding the Kanawha Valley. Finding the bridge destroyed, the men crossed over the surging waters by means of rope ferry.

IT WAS RAINING fitfully and then steadily as the troops entered the Gauley Bridge area. The band struck up "The Rocky Road to Dublin." Riding ahead, General Crook could hear the pointed remarks of his men, calling for a halt and griping about their sopping clothes. If General Crook could not hear, it was certainly no fault of the men who were doing their best to make him hear their loud comments that it was time to halt.

Finally, General Crook directed that the division, led by Hechler's company, file into a bivouac area. Only then did one of Hechler's buddies, Joe Schofield suddenly change his plea, and cry: "For God's sake, let's go on! I'm just getting my second wind!!"

Water dripping from his hat and clothes, General Crook sat on his horse and listened to Joe Schofield for a minute, as the rest of the men went into bivouac. The usually poker-faced Crook, veteran of many battles with the Indians, suddenly broke into quiet laughter. For Hechler and his friends, this was worth getting rain-soaked.

27. Corporal Hechler

Trouble with Strays — Trouble with Furloughs

FOR A MAN in the Army, a battlefield promotion is a great glory, and nothing can exceed that first promotion from buck private to corporal. After the bloody battle of Antietam, Private Hechler became Corporal Hechler, and there was great rejoicing in the Hechler household in Marietta.

"You want to know how I like my new office," Cpl. Hechler wrote his sister in Marietta. "Well, to tell the truth," he wrote with thinly veiled modesty, "I would rather have none at all, but after I have got into it I shall try and do my duty. I got into it like some others when I couldn't help it."

From Clarksburg and Summersville, the men of the 36th Ohio Volunteer Infantry Regiment in November of 1862 marched down into the Kanawha Valley and once again took up their positions near Charleston. Here they braced themselves for the winter, and in his first letter Cpl. Hechler wrote on November 21, 1862:

> My Dear Sister:
>
> We are now encamped just below Charleston on the right hand of the Elk River, and on a beautiful bottom. We will probably stay here this winter, but we don't know yet. We have only

two Sibley tents to a company, and the most of us have to stay in small tents without fire. It is rather cool lodging these cold, rainy days. The river has commenced rising. A few small boats are running up at far as Camp Piatt, 10 miles above Charleston.

I have received the stamps you sent by Captain Kelly and the little bags you sent by Mr. Turner. The bags will come in handy when we start out again.

Captain Jewett Palmer has returned with three men of our company that went home on their own account. Two of them are in Charleston jail with handcuffs on, and the other one is sick at the hospital.

You said you were very much gratified with the report that Captain Palmer gave you of Brother John and me. Well, perhaps you are proud of your brothers, and your pride makes you only look at the best side of the question.

There is some talk about Captain Palmer not being a good Captain or he would have been promoted. Whoever started such talk knows nothing about military matters, for it can hardly come from his enemies because he has none in the regiment.

You want to know what to do about the money I sent you. Well I have sent it to you for safe keeping, and that's all you ought to do with it.

Has Brother John sent for the Marietta Register yet? If he has not, I wish you would subscribe for me for the term of six months and have the paper directed to me, because I would like to find out what is going on about Marietta.

There is a rumor in camp now that we are going to Point Pleasant in a few days, but nothing positive.

I have not been troubled with the rheumatism since I wrote to you from Summersville, and hope it is all cured.

Your loving brother, George

EVEN IN A WELL-DISCIPLINED unit such as General Crook had trained, there was occasional trouble with A.W.O.L.'s. On one of his furloughs home in Marietta, Hechler's company commander, Captain Jewett Palmer, rounded up several "strays" as revealed in the letter quoted above. Here is how Palmer's Marietta sweetheart, Miss Saida M. Scott, described it in a note to her mother and father in the fall of 1862:

"Dan Goodman came up to see about his brother Nat who has deserted from Jewett's company. Jewett told him if his brother went back of his own free will he would probably escape punishment but if he waited till he had to take him he would be punished as a deserter."

Soon the men in camp at the confluence of the Elk and Kanawha rivers in Charleston began to get ready for the long winter ahead. They picked their camp on a fine level stretch of river bottom, on the site where soldiers in the French and Indian Wars had received the first lands patented under Dinwoodie's proclamation of 1754 for their wartime service. The men went out to collect timbers, dug trenching, put up walls and dug in for protection against wintry blasts. The old regimental commander, General Crook-now the division commander-took over a commodious brick house in the center of Charleston as his headquarters. The remainder of the camp was soon labeled "Camp Crook" by the men.

WRITING HOME EARLY in December from Charleston, Corporal Hechler noted that with Christmas approaching the men were getting restive again about their furloughs:

> My Dear Sister:
>
> We are still here near Charleston, have our quarters fixed up, and expect to stay here this winter. We have the promise of furloughs this winter, but I shall not be able to come home in time to spend the Holidays in Marietta. Perhaps I shall not come before Spring.
>
> There was some trouble in the Regiment about furloughs. The men, or some of them, wanted to have the General do as they said about it, but he was not willing. Three of them have started from here, but others were sent after them, and if they are brought back the punishment they will receive will perhaps cure all the rest from doing anything like it hereafter.

Some of the men wrote a letter to General Crook, signed 36th Regiment, about furloughs. He came to our camp the next evening and told the company officers about it, telling them at the same time that he thought ten or fifteen days would be sufficient to bring the 36th up, in drill and discipline to the old standard, and they could have furloughs, but they need not try and scare him into giving them furloughs for they could not do it.

Mr. Barber (the quartermaster) is going home tomorrow or the day after, and I shall send this letter by him.

The weather looks beautiful today, but very warm. The nights are very cold and there is still some snow on the ground. We have to drill twice each day and dress parade every evening.

I am still well, and so is Brother John, and I hope this will find you the same.

Your affectionate brother, George

28. A Crisis in the 36th

A Trying Affair — Mud of Charleston
Wilson Deputized — Two Cheers and a Groan

WINTERING NEAR Charleston, W.Va. at the close of 1862 proved to be as comfortable as could be expected for Hechler's regiment, once they learned how to cope with the "gumbo soup" mud. The rain and snow, the churning of the wagons and hundreds of marching feet, soon turned the encampment almost into a quagmire.

Out of the mud of Charleston came a new disaffection which threatened to tear apart the 36th Ohio Volunteer Infantry Regiment. This proud and well-disciplined unit, which had covered itself with glory at Lewisburg and Antietam, suddenly found itself mired down in dissension. With the promotion of General George Crook, the regiment's first commander, and the fatal wounding of Lt. Col. Melvin Clarke in the Battle of South Mountain the regimental command went to Lt. Col. Ebenezer B. Andrews.

In the eyes of the officers and men, Col. Andrews was a top-notch staff officer but left something to be desired as a leader on the field of battle. Here is how one of Hechler's close friends, Sgt. John T. Booth described the command situation:

"Col. Andrews in civilian life was and is a man of honorable and distinguished points, a man of high intelligence and ability. I was a student in his class. In the formation of the regiment he worked strenuously for the good of the regiment. He did perhaps more than any other single individual. He helped us obtain our crowning glory, George Crook, and he was instrumental in obtaining for us our splendid Enfield rifles. But as a military leader, he was a failure, flat and absolute. The dumbest, thickest-headed man in the regiment knew and felt the incubus of Andrews' presence as commander. It was prayerfully hoped that for the good of the regiment that Col. Andrews would resign his commission. Col. Andrews wanted out, but he desired to go out with honor, and was averse to being pushed out while under a cloud. The men of the regiment eventually took up the cudgels and were as outspoken as they dared to. If he persists in remaining in command, I very greatly fear for the command's future. He knows all this. We know all this. He knows that we know all this. And we know that he knows that we know all this."

LT. AUGUSTUS T. WARD, who later succeeded Capt. Jewett Palmer as Hechler's company commander, kept a diary of this trying affair which contained the following entries in the winter of 1862:

Nov. 21, 1862: The line officers of the regiment got up a petition asking Col. Andrews to resign his commission. Every company officer signed except Captain Barker. Captain Kelly handed the petition to Col. Andrews this morning. He read it without a word or change of countenance, and then told him he would "see him again about the matter."

Nov. 22: Col. Andrews has given us no word yet about the resignation. We are bound to push to the last extremity. Dame Nature neither fashioned him on lines a la militaire, or thrust upon him the ability to give correctly the simplest military commands.

Nov. 26: The company officers held a meeting to deliberate on the Col. Andrews question. He has positively refused to resign. By a unanimous vote we are to hand in our own resignations tomorrow. I love the service of my country, but I go with the rest.

Nov. 27: Every officer in the line sent in his resignation this morning.

Nov. 30: Well, this evening General Crook sent for Captains Barker and Henry in regard to the Andrews question. He told them the matter must be settled, and be settled, immediately. They had a considerable conversation during which Captain Henry was chief spokesman. Henry explained the causes all over again and the unanimity of feeling on the part of the line officers. General Crook told them to see and talk with Colonel Andrews about it that very evening. They came back and waited on Col. Andrews but after at least an hour's consultation he still refused to resign. He wants us to "wait and let him try" and then if he can't succeed he'll resign", etc., but Captain Henry gave him fully to understand that he or the officers of the line must leave. After the confab was over, Capt. Henry came to Captain Palmer's quarters where all the officers of the line were assembled to hear the results of the two interviews. All that now remains is for us to push on our resignations which we resolved unanimously to do forthwith. If the "powers that be" think Col. Andrews worth more than the 36th Regiment, let them accept our resignations and we will go home and the 36th will not be far behind.

DEC 2: THE OFFICERS held a meeting in Captain Nye's quarters this morning and deputized Capt. Wilson to wait on General Crook with the following proposition: "That if he, the general, will give us the solemn assurance that we shall be rid of Col. Andrews by January 1st we will withdraw our resignations and do our duties to the utmost, but if not then we wish that the resignations be attended to at once." The Captain waited on General Crook and arranged the following plan to which all acceded: that Col. Andrews go to Washington, D. C. with a recommendation that he be reassigned as a staff officer. This leaves the regiment in command of Lt. Col. Devol in whom the regiment has confidence and respect.

Dec. 4: Lt. Stearns went over to Col. Andrews' tent to get his resignation. When he refused to deliver it up, we called a meeting and deputized Capt. Kelly to see General Crook again. The General said that we must reinstate the colonel to his former reputation. This we cannot do and we resolved unanimously never to apologize for our course.

Dec. 7: General Crook issued an order that no furloughs would be issued until the troops were thoroughly disciplined and effective.

Lt. Benjamin F. Stearns

Feb. 10: General Crook called the officers of the 36th together and made them a speech this afternoon. He said the discipline must be brought back to the old standard, and that our resignations would not be accepted by him. The officers didn't like the speech very well.

On February 23, 1863, Cpl. Hechler, in response to an inquiry from his sister Kate in Marietta, wrote what was the general feeling of the enlisted men in the 36th Regiment:

> I do not know where Col. Andrews is now, nor can, I find out. I have not seen him since we came to this place. He has preferred charges against Captains Kelly and Nye. They were court martialed last week, but I have not heard the charge nor sentence of either yet. Andrews had them both under arrest but their companies threatened to leave the regiment, and actually went on shore. (It was as we came down the Ohio River on our

> way here) till General Crook went to them and promised them their officers. They refused to go back on board, but finally they gave General Crook two cheers and Andrews one groan then went aboard. If the friends of Andrews think him a good officer they had better come and serve under him, for the 36th certainly never will.

The crisis in the 36th Regiment was finally resolved when Col. Andrews left the Army in the spring of 1863. But these were agonizing months for both General Crook and his officers and men. General Crook could not for disciplinary reasons immediately accede to the demands of his company officers, nor could he afford to lose a loyal and courageous corps of line officers who had proven their worth in combat. The difficult affair was finally resolved, and Hechler's regiment went on to rebuild its spirit and discipline until once again the regiment went into combat to write another glorious chapter in Civil War annals.

29. Christmas, 1862

Camp Crook — Move to Nashville

ONCE THE COMMAND situation had been cleared up in the 36th Ohio Volunteer Infantry Regiment, Cpl. Hechler found his unit again ready for any combat mission which was assigned.

Christmas of 1862 was spent at "Camp Crook", that muddy and rain-swept bottom near Charleston, W. Va. It was the second Christmas away from their Marietta home for Cpl. Hechler and his brother, Pvt. John Hechler. On January 4, 1863, Cpl. Hechler wrote to his sister Kate in Marietta:

> My Dear Sister:
>
> I received the box and letter you sent by Mr. Barber last night and was glad to get something good for a New Year's gift from you. I have not opened any of the jars as yet, but they are all safe.
>
> I gave the package to Mr. Barber, who wanted to keep it for him, as Mr. Corey is now gone hone on a furlough and they both belong to the band.
>
> I have thought about writing to you at Christmas and New Year, but did not do it. I was not doing anything but staying in camp, and I enjoyed well enough on both Christmas and New Year, a great deal better than I did last year. I was well and hearty, for which I thank God who has watched over me in all danger and kept me from evil to see the sun of another year. But if it is His will that I shall live much longer, His will be done. But shall we go unprepared to stand before His throne? I hope not!
>
> We now have visitors here in our mess, and plenty of good

things to eat. Because we live together in our mess like a family, if one has anything, we all have it.

The weather today is fine but cool. We have not had much snow yet this winter, but a considerable amount of dry, cold, more of the latter than I have seen for some time. In consequence of this, the health of our troops here is excellent, only a few are in the regimental hospital and none of them in dangerous condition.

There was a rumor here last week that our regiment was to go down south before long, but I do not believe it yet. If we stay here, and there will be as many furloughs given as there are now.

Give my thanks and best respects to Mrs. Whitney for her kindness in sending us such things as are good to eat. I hope she may be blessed with health and appetite as to enjoy life as I now do.

From your loving brother, George

From Marietta, a young music teacher named Miss Saida M. Scott, the sweetheart of Hechler's company commander, Capt. Jewett Palmer, wrote about her own New Year in this way:

My Dearest Jewett:

I was invited out to tea with General Cox and his staff on New Year's Eve, but Uncle Ned was here, and I thought he was more to see than the General. I didn't accept the invitation. It was quite a large party and all the Big Straps were there. Uncle Ned left about nine o'clock and I could have gone then as many did not go until ten o'clock. I was just a little bit sorry the next day that I did not as they all had such a good time, but it is just as well as it is.

I have made the acquaintance of three of General Cox's staff. They are very agreeable and intelligent, but I think they would better be where they could be doing more good instead of here receiving the attention of the ladies, being feted and flattered while the poor soldiers are off so nobly fighting for our rights. I was introduced to one of them four times by different people, and we feel very well acquainted. He is a handsome fellow but too conceited.

How I wish you were here to enjoy all these parties with me. It does not seem right to go and have such good times while you are way off there. But when you come home, we will make it up, won't we dear? Meanwhile, don't let any of those Charleston belles captivate my property.

I send some papers by John Booth to keep you from getting the blues.

Your own affectionate Saida

AS THE MONTH of January, 1863 wore on, it became apparent that soon the Fighting Thirty-sixth would be moved out of their winter quarters and toward the front of active fighting. The Army of the Cumberland in Tennessee had suffered heavily in six months' of severe combat and needed reinforcements. Hence, it was decided to send the 36th down the Kanawha River and then down the Ohio river and up the Tennessee to Nashville. Here is how Cpl. Hechler described the situation on the eve of his departure from Charleston, W. Va., in a letter dated January 23, 1863:

My Dear Sister:

I received your letter dated the 16th a few days ago, and was glad to hear that you were yet well and able to work, but still you complain of your hand trembling much and I fear you do not enjoy your health. I am well now. I weigh heavier than I have before. The health of the whole regiment is good.

We have good quarters here at Charleston and all are fixed up well. The mud is getting very deep around here in camp, and the roads are getting very bad in West Virginia. But this will not trouble us much longer, as an order was issued this evening for four regiments, including the 36th, to get ready to embark aboard transports soon, provided with ten days' ration, and if on the way a boat is fired into it shall land immediately and engage any enemy in sight. This is a little like Crook's generalship, and seems to point us to Dixie.

We have had much rain and snow up here on the Kanawha, and the river is high, or rather in good condition only for boats to run. We do not know when we will have to start yet, perhaps about Sunday morning.

We do not like to leave here because we have good quarters, and our rations regularly, besides a prospect of getting furloughs. But this we must give up now and think no more of it, as we will scarcely have another chance before the close of this war.

And if it should not be our fortune to meet again on this earth, I hope that we may be prepared to meet in a better place where there is no pain nor sorrow nor care, and where our good Mother has long gone before us.

But I have no more to write. Give my love to all inquiring folks. John is well.

I hope to hear from you soon in some other place. Bidding you good night and pleasant dreams, I remain

Your affectionate brother, George

30. The 36th Joins Army of the Cumberland

Red House Landing — Camp of Nashville

THE ARMY OF THE Cumberland, commanded by General Rosecrans, had been somewhat battered in Tennessee and so it welcomed the news that General Crook was bringing his Kanawha Division down from Charleston to join them early in 1863.

Cpl. Hechler barely had time to dash off a quick note to his sister Kate in Marietta when the troops got on the steamers at Red House Landing in Putnam County for the boat trip down the Kanawha River, His note read:

> Dear Sister:
>
> Enclosed you will find 40 dollars. I send 30 and brother John 10. Keep John's till you hear from him. You may loan mine if you find a good and safe place.
>
> Our company is just being paid aboard the *Liberty*. We go on the *Odd Fellow* and will start soon.
>
> I shall try and send this by Mr. Barber.
>
> John is well, and so am I.
>
> Goodbye, from
>
> Your Ever loving brother George

Down the Kanawha River the steamers puffed, and after many delays they landed at Point Pleasant about 10:30 on the morning of January 27. The next afternoon they reached Cincinnati, and on the afternoon of the 29th they had arrived in Louisville.

The trip was not altogether a pleasant one for the men, who were jammed tightly together on the overcrowded boats. The fight in the top command of the 36th Regiment over Col. Andrews had not left morale very high either. Here is how Cpl. Hechler described the trip to Nashville: in his first letter home to Marietta after reaching Nashville:

> February 8, 1863
>
> My Dear Sister:
>
> As we have arrived at our present place of destination, I shall try and let you know that I am yet well and I hope this will find you the same.
>
> We landed here yesterday evening after being on the boats nearly two weeks, but are not off the boats yet and there is no sign of our going off today yet. The weather has been cold ever since we left the Kanawha. But for that we might have had a pleasant trip, but it was too cold to stay outside any length of time, and the cabin and engine room were as crowded as they could be, so we could scarcely all sit down. There are three companies of us on the *Odd Fellow*—over 200 men.
>
> Yesterday was a pleasant day, and at times we could see nearly the whole fleet. There were over fifty transports, all but two or three loaded with troops, and six gunboats came up the Cumberland from Fort Donelson in one fleet. We arrived at Fort Donelson the night after the fight and stopped one day. When we left, our men had found and buried nearly 200 dead Rebels, besides a number of wounded. It was a dear raid for the Rebels.
>
> Have you received the money yet I sent by Mr. Barber? I started $30 for safe keeping and Brother John $10, but he will tell you what to do with his. We started a box of clothing from Charleston. I do not know whether you will get it or not, but if you do, each piece is marked. One overcoat belongs to John, one to Martin Schwartz, and one to me. I do not know whether there is anything else in it or not besides a blacking brush, which belongs to me.
>
> Ed Doudle has left us. The sky is dark and cloudy today, but the air is getting warmer and I hope the snow will soon be off the

ground, as it will not be pleasant to leave the boat now and camp on top of the snow.

From your loving brother, George

On February 20, 1863, Cpl. Hechler wrote in a little more detail about the 36th Regiment's camp near Nashville:

My Dear Sister:

I shall now try and write a few lines to you this afternoon. I have been looking for a letter from you for some time, but have not gotten any yet since we left western Virginia.

We are camped here now about three miles south of Nashville. The country is beautiful, rolling, and is owned by wealthy planters, all of whom live in large two and three-story brick buildings, well-finished outside. I have never seen inside any of them, therefore do not know how they look inside. Rebel Colin McNairy, who was killed at the last fight at Fort Donelson, owns two square miles adjoining the farm we are camped on. The soil is a black limestone loam nearly two feet deep and very rich, but I do not believe that there will be much of anything raised in this neighborhood as nearly all the fences are destroyed. Our camp is in a wood, or rather grove, as all the underbrush is cleared out and heavy greensward covers the ground.

We have had a great deal of rain since we came here, but only one or two slight frosts, and the roads are getting very bad. Last night we had a hard storm without rain. It carried off my hat, away over the tents, but this morning when I went to hunt for it, I found another one and took it. Whether the former owner has found any yet I do not know.

Today the sun is shining warm and the ground is getting dry fast. In a few days the roads will be good and we will in all probability soon have to move. Our camp is only about 400 yards from the railroad running to Franklin, which is nearly repaired to that point. We have had orders for several days to keep ourselves in readiness to march at a moment's notice, and yesterday all the men who are not able to march were sent to town. There is a strong force encamped now about this town.

Have you seen Edward Doudle yet, or did he not go home?
There are eleven gone from our camp since we left Charleston.
Brother John is well, and so am I yet. I remain
Your affectionate brother George

The year 1863 was the year when the state of West Virginia was born. For Cpl. Hechler it was a year torn with trial and heartaches, culminating in the Battles of Chickamauga and Chattanooga where his Brother John was missing in action.

31. On the Road to Chattanooga

About the Fanny Barker — Grant on the Move
Ohio Companies Surrender

EARLY IN 1863, the 36th Ohio Volunteer Infantry Regiment left West Virginia by steamboat down the Ohio River and thence across to Tennessee and Georgia where some of the bloodiest fighting of the war occurred at Chattanooga and Chickamauga. From Nashville, Corporal Hechler wrote his sister in Marietta on February 23, 1863:

> I do not know whether you can read this letter or not, as I have no ink to write with, and a poor place to write. We are aboard the *Fanny Barker*, a sternwheeler, at present. We came here yesterday. The 4th Regiment that left Kanawha, or General Crook's brigade, and one battery of artillery are aboard boats, lying here at Nashville, but there is no sign of our leaving today yet. I do not know where we are going; some say Cumberland Gap is our destination.
>
> Brother John is well and so am I. Ed Doudle left the boat without permission, with the intention of deserting, and is marked a deserter. Major Adney is not drowned but is well. The report started at Louisville where he crossed the river and another skiff upset at the time, which was seen from our boat and believed to be the one the Major was in, but nobody drowned.
>
> You had better leave the money in the bank till after we are paid off again, unless you find a reliable person just wanting so small a sum, or if you need any yourself do not be afraid to touch it.
>
> From your loving brother, George

For the next three months, the 36th remained near Carthage, then moved to Murfreesboro, and then on to the clash of arms at Chattanooga.

From his camp near Carthage on March 2, 1863, Corporal Hechler wrote in considerable detail about the experiences of his regiment, more than half of which was drawn from the Wood County-Washington County area:

> My Dear Sister:
>
> As we have again arrived at a camp where we will perhaps stay a few days or weeks, I shall try and write a few lines and try and let you know where we are. I am yet well, and so is Brother John, and I hope this will find you enjoying good health. I wrote a few lines to you after we had marching orders. I don't know whether you got them or not and it is doubtful about this as Morgan is hovering about here conscripting men, and it is supposed he has already captured one of our mail carriers due last night from Gallatin, near the Kentucky line.
>
> We started Tuesday, after getting on the boats Sunday. The 11th, 36th, 89th and 72nd Ohio and have not seen any cavalry yet, since we left Nashville. We came up to Carthage Thursday evening. Friday morning our Company G was ordered to search the town for Rebel soldiers, but did not find anyone; one had been taken the evening before. He first claimed to be a conscript, but some of his acquaintances called him 'Major,' and it is generally believed this was his real rank in Morgan's Confederate thieving army.
>
> Saturday morning we came off the boats and pitched our tents about one mile from the river and opposite Carthage. The four regiments of Ohio troops are scattered over considerable ground, through the woods and along the side hills. The ground near the river is very broken, hardly any level, but the most of it can be cultivated and a great deal of it is now. A few miles from the river the country is more even as seen from the hills. Sunday morning General Crook sent an order for Companies G and D of the 36th to report to him at his headquarters with arms immediately. His headquarters was still on the steamboat *Emma Duncan*.

General Braxton Bragg

General John H. Morgan

When we reached the river, the Crescent City had steam up and we went aboard. Then she started upstream and turned into Cane Creek. We were all ordered to keep inside the boat, so we could not see anything on shore. After running about ten or twelve miles, the boat landed at a crossing where there was a ferryboat, and some men were sent on shore.

I was in one squad that went to the farm of one Widow Allen-all bitter Secesh. There were several young ladies at the house trying to scare us out by telling that Morgan had promised to be back that very day. Upon hearing this, Captain Palmer turned to go, saying that if Morgan were coming he would leave. But we had found out all we wanted to know, so we went back to the boat. Yet they stood on the bank not a little surprised when the steamer passed the house going further upstream after another boat we had discovered and pursued. We now found that we had been sent to get the ferryboats of the neighborhood, as some of Morgan's men had been crossing the river there nearly every day. They cannot cross the high river without boats, and it is not likely the water will be down for two months low enough to ford the creek and Cumberland River in this neighborhood.

General Bragg, crossed half his army over the Cumberland here at Carthage last summer when he made his raid into Kentucky, and nearly all the prisoners he took from Rosecrans in the Murfreesboro fight after being paroled passed through here on their way north.

There are but few Union people in this part of Tennessee. Most all of the men are gone, however, into the Confederate Army, so we could hardly expect any sympathy from their relatives or friends while we are driving them still further from home.

Wheat and corn are plentiful still in this country, but everything else is scarce. Salt is twelve dollars per bushel and other things, except the two above–named articles, expensive in proportion.

This morning we had the heaviest frost I have yet seen in Tennessee. But the weather today was warm enough to sit in the sun and be comfortable.

There are a good many citizens coming in today. Some say that General Bragg has issued an order for all of them to move southward. Others report General Bragg will tomorrow or the next day attack us with a large force. I hope if he does come he will be as well entertained as General Heth was at Lewisburg!

But it's nearly dress parade time, and I must close this letter.

Your ever loving brother, George

IN THE SPRING of 1863, Ulysses S. Grant and his armies were moving into the heart of the South's great cotton empire and sweeping onward toward Vicksburg. Slaughtered at Fredericksburg, the Army of the Potomac met disaster again at Chancellorsville. The Civil War had not yet reached its decisive phase.

In West Virginia the Confederate forces began to regain the initiative. A West Virginia delegation called on President Lincoln to ask for protection against Rebel raids. But the Union troops formerly in West Virginia, including Corporal Hechler, had a more important mission in Tennessee as they mobilized for the strikes toward Chattanooga.

From camp near Carthage, Tenn., Corporal Hechler wrote his sister in Marietta on March 9, 1863:

> Since I wrote my last letter to you, we have had a little trouble here, and have scarcely rested a whole day in camp. The same evening after I started my letter our pickets were fired upon. Companies G and E under command of Captain Jewett Palmer were ordered out to find out what was the matter and support the pickets if necessary, but the pickets had driven the Rebels off. There were about 15 or 20 Rebel cavalry and nearly half as many on the picket post.
>
> Next day we moved our camp, about a half mile by the road, or about 500 yards across the hill. On the 4th of this month, about 6 p.m., we started the whole regiment and marched till 1 a.m.-our Company G again in advance-with our blankets over our shoulders and looking as ragged as we could make ourselves appear, trying to pass for Confederate scouts. In this, we succeeded in all but one or two instances among the citizens. We did not meet any armed Rebels. We halted at 1 o'clock in the morning, and laid down, but could not sleep much as the weather was too cold. It had been snowing the day before, and cleared up toward evening. The snow froze hard and so did the ground, and did not feel very comfortable.
>
> About daylight the next morning, we started and were soon in Rome. But it does not look like a great city after all. We were there too late, as the 11th Regiment had taken a shorter route and beat us there by about 25 minutes. They only found a few men in the place, whom they took prisoners. Rome is down the Cumberland River, and about eight miles distant by the nearest route. We had to march 18 miles to reach the place, and had to come all the way around back again, while the 11th Regiment came by the nearer road. We came back on the afternoon of the 6th.
>
> Yesterday about noon we heard heavy firing and soon after a messenger came in with the news that our forage train had been attacked by Rebel cavalry and probably captured. Four companies were ordered out again, Company G among them, under command of Captain Jewett Palmer. We marched nearly eight miles in one hour and fifteen minutes, but arrived one half hour

too late. The guard and two companies of the 11th Ohio Regiment had surrendered without firing one shot to a force about three times their number. They lost two wounded which the Rebels, in their haste to get off, left lay. On our arrival, they had been picked up, we found, and cared for by Parson Bowen's family, who lives there. Parson himself is a fugitive. He returned with us from Nashville, but has not been at home yet.

Our loss was 30 men with their arms, 18 wagons and about 100 head of horses and mules. Many of the men escaped and came to camp, but these are not included in the loss. They were completely taken by surprise and it is said the officer in command had gone to a house to get his dinner at the time.

Today again is a warm and beautiful day and our clothes are getting dry fast. We had to wade a creek yesterday, over knee deep, and coming back it rained and hailed hard nearly all the time. When I came into the tent all my clothes were not any too dry after wringing them out. Some of our men are out again today, and others are working on breastworks, but most of Company G is really laying in their tents trying to rest or write letters.

Your loving brother, George.

IN HIS NEXT LETTER to his Sister Kate, Corporal Hechler elaborated a little on the incident of the surrender of several companies of the 11th Ohio Regiment. "The men of the 11th Regiment are good soldiers," he wrote, "and I have since found out that some of them fired their guns before being taken, and wounded two of the Rebels slightly. But the officer in command, Captain Johnson of company K, seems to have lost his senses and saw nothing but visions of a southern prison or something worse. The talk goes that he said as soon as being attacked: 'Boys, we are done up!' Certain it is that he never once gave an order to fire. I have not met with anyone yet in the regiment that I was acquainted with, as the circle of my acquaintances was very limited."

This was a very trying period for the Union soldiers in Tennessee. The spring rains, cold, mud and discomfort were bad enough. After the Battle of Murfreesboro in the early months of 1863, —

General Rosecrans was licking his wounds and regrouping for further attacks down the Cumberland River toward Chattanooga. But perhaps the most disturbing news to the Union soldiers were rumors of discontent on the home front. Vallandigham and the advocates of a quick end to hostilities were making headway in Ohio. They were holding enthusiastic meetings in Marietta, and this news as much as the danger of enemy bullets kept the soldiers of the Army of the Cumberland deeply worried.

32. Lively Correspondence, 1863

Love Affair — Deserters Return — "Copperheads"

SPRING CAME TO Parkersburg and Marietta in 1863, and with it the deepening of the love between a Marietta music teacher named Saida M. Scott and the dashing young company commander of Corporal Hechler's infantry company—later to become four-time Mayor of Marietta: Jewett Palmer.

"My own dearest Jewett," wrote Saida, "I am so sorry, dearest, that you are feeling so unwell. I wish I could be with you to nurse you and comb your hair. I wouldn't pull it any more but would comb it so nicely for you and wouldn't you think the magical touch of my fingers would cure you? I am sorry that you are going to move, right in the way of danger too, but it may be best for we need to crush this rebellion before it gains any more strength. I pray God to turn away the Rebel's ball from you and bring you out of the war unharmed, and soon, and I have faith enough to believe God will hear my prayer."

With Jewett Palmer's company in camp near Carthage, Tennessee, Corporal Hechler wrote on March 28, 1863:

> Spring is about to clothe nature here with her finest garments, grass begins to spring up, wild flowers bloom (but there is not much chance for me to get many of them, as we are scarcely allowed to leave our regimental camps). Peach trees are past bloom and the woods begin to assume a green hue.
>
> Last night we had the hardest rain and thunderstorm I have yet seen in Tennessee. The water leaked through our tent nearly like a sieve. Our blankets became wet and the water ran through

under us. I lay still till morning, but after I got up I built a fire in the stove and sat down close to it to get my clothes dry, which I finally succeeded in doing.

Our regiment has not lost any yet since we have been here. There are two or three cases of smallpox in the division, one from our regiment, but they are all nearly well again from what I can find out.

Today the first battalion of the 1st Middle Tennessee Cavalry, Colonel Stokes' Regiment, came in and are now camped near us. They are a set of fine and soldierly-looking men, but are poorly mounted, many have no horses at all, but we can supply part of them from what we captured. They started last Tuesday evening, under a drenching rain, and came back again the next day in the afternoon with 34 prisoners, 8 wagons and about 80 head of horses and mules. Wednesday night the 36th started out, about half of Company G mounted. I had not the pleasure of being with them, as I had been detailed for picket duty in the morning and was not relieved in time to go. I call it a pleasure, for in spite of the hardship there are almost always many amusing little incidents and accidents which happen to keep us cheerful or most of the time merry.

Some of the boys captured a mail carrier and mail, among it several papers from Dixie. Captain Jewett Palmer has one copy of the Chattanooga Daily Rebel, March 22, 1863. It contains an account of the destruction of the gunboat "Indianola" by the Rebels. The cause of it was a big scare from an old flat-bottomed boat which our men had started from above in the evening, and was drifting down the river. Several barrels had been put on the top of each other to represent a smoke-stack, and logs had been placed on it for guns. But the 'heroic' Rebels thought the barrels a revolving turret of the Ericson (Monitor) pattern, opened their batteries on them, ran the Queen the West away as fast as possible and blew up the Indianola. Another piece speaks about southern women. It says a few days ago about 20 women, all decently and some of them elegantly dressed, wearing gold ear lobes and breast pins, assembled in Atlanta, Georgia, went to some of the grocery stores in that city and took bacon at one, meal at another, and other articles, paying such prices for them as they saw fit, saying they had money as they were making clothing for the government, but they would decline to pay the customarily exorbitant prices for articles. Perhaps this is the heroic conduct of southern ladies so long prophesied by the southern merchants. The newspaper has besides a long letter in it about the wanton destruction of property, especially fences, by the Yankees and stragglers, and by their own men in search of something to eat. The detail uses a great many big words, as it seems exceedingly hard for the editor to fill his half sheet, nearly as large as half of the Marietta Register.

Wishing you a good evening, I remain
Your loving brother, George

IN HIS NEXT LETTER on April 14, 1863, Corporal Hechler informed his sister in Marietta that:

> The Company—or Brigade, rather—is out on expedition. They crossed the Cumberland River yesterday about noon. There were many rumors yesterday concerning the move. Some had eight or ten thousand Rebel prisoners crossing or across the river down at Rome, and a strong force above there had not half as many. I was on picket duty at the river, and when I came to camp this morning all but a few sick members of Company G had gone, but nobody knew which way. The probability is that they have gone toward Gallatin to clear the road of guerrillas, as Captain Jewett Palmer had on butternut clothes when they started. This is the second scout I have missed lately on account of being on duty, although I should have liked to go as the weather for the past two weeks has been all that could be desired. This morning we had about two hours of very mild rain, but now the sun is shining brightly again, and the birds are singing as sweetly as ever in the woods, among the green trees-for some of the trees are nearly as green as Spring will ever make them.
>
> Some of our absentees, or better, 'deserters,' as we call them in this city, have returned. They nearly all have been treated coldly or contemptuously and if they have any shame left are certainly

now ashamed of their former conduct. Captain Cherrington's business, as near as I can find out, is to gather up all he can find of them and bring them back to the Regiment.

We have no first or second lieutenant now, but will soon have, I think. Colonel Andrews has been ordered, by special order from General Rosecrans, to report to Nashville and there await further orders...

The health of the troops at present here is good, with the exception of the 92nd Ohio. They do not appear to be getting much better. Three of them were buried yesterday evening. One man of company H of our regiment has had the smallpox, but he is well again and nobody else but a few Negroes who are working in camp (most of them who came in lately) took smallpox.

It is again raining. I shall close this letter. Brother John will perhaps tell you when he writes again where Company G was and why they did, as he is along.

Write soon to
Your affectionate brother, George

GEORGE HECHLER WAS a rock-ribbed Republican to the core. He was deeply dedicated to President Abraham Lincoln. In most respects, Corporal Hechler in his Union Blues during the Civil War maintained an even-tempered disposition, taking the bitter with the sweet with good humor. But one topic made his blood boil: the wartime dissenters in Parkersburg, Marietta, and the Ohio Valley.

The critics of the war soon became known as "copperheads," and since many of Lincoln's critics were Democrats. George Hechler turned his ire against the Democrats, Chief among the Democratic leaders who opposed the war was Ohio Congressman Clement L. Vallandigham—a man Hechler regarded as a traitor who was undermining his country through his subversive activities.

Vallandigham was due to speak in Marietta at a great mass meeting, but was thwarted by lack of river transportation. Thus it was that Corporal Hechler in a white heat of rage penned these acid lines from his tent in the field with the Army of the Cumberland, April 14, 1863:

Clement L. Vallandigham

I suppose the Democrats of Marietta thought it really despotic for the Government to charter the only boat on the Muskingum River and then refuse to carry their great Chief (Vallandigham), so that he could not be present at a great meeting in Marietta. The meeting had for its object the destruction of that same Government. So this great "Statesman and Patriot," who has suffered 'persecution' (as he himself claims) for the sake of the 'liberties' of the people, has to break his word. In saying he was persecuted. Vallandigham must have reference to the time when the boys of the first and second Ohio Regiments prepared a rope for him near Washington City. Had they succeeded in catching and hanging him, they would have done more service to their country and contributed a great share to the putting down people in this County, and I have never had the good luck to get to any yet, but some of the Secesh ladies have treated us as well as they could, setting good tables and talking about the state of affairs generally. Others would not give us anything but some poor corn dodgers and a little poor bacon, but plenty of sour looks. There are some fine plantations and many of the planters are putting in big crops of corn, but some of them will not be able to work them much because their Negro boys are running away. Many others will not raise much, some for want of teams and their Negroes. There is scarcely a good horse or mule now in the country, except in the Army. We brought in some sixteen or eighteen head of them, all we could find worth anything, belonging to the Rebels.

The purpose of the expedition was to find out what citizens, if any, had been engaged in robbing our mail, as it had been robbed three or four times since we have been here. We found two that were willing to go and help take it, but could get no evidence that they ever had helped, so the Captain let them go, but made them promise first to report themselves at Headquarters, and one of them came in yesterday about noon. The other will hardly come, but it does not make much difference as we know him now and will know how to treat him if ever caught again. We do not care about keeping prisoners.

Morgan has had another thumping again, losing what stores he had, and a number of men, but he, himself has taken to the mountains, some Rebel citizens say, even leaving his wife behind him. About ten days ago a detachment of his force captured about eighteen of Stokes' cavalry, killing over forty head of beef cattle and one load of sutler goods. On the road between Gallatin and Carthage, they killed two sutlers and one Chaplain, piled their bodies under the wagon, and after taking out of it what they wanted, set it on fire, nearly burning up the bodies before another detachment of our cavalry came up.

The prisoners they took were all recaptured on a train going toward Chattanooga, and have returned to try their hand at it again. Some of their captors were also captured and I hope will be punished according to their deeds.

Your loving brother, George

33. Deserters Tell Wild Stories

New Commander — Sixteen Deserters Will Hang Spy

LINCOLN EARLY IN MAY was asked for a pass to Richmond. "Well," said Abe, "I would be very happy to oblige you, if my passes were respected: but the fact is sir, I have, within the past two years given passes to 250,000 men to go to Richmond, and not one has got there yet!"

On April 20, 1863, President Lincoln struck a great blow for the Union by issuing the proclamation admitting West Virginia into the Union. But the embattled forces of the new free state were still having grave difficulties with Rebel raiders.

From the Army of the Cumberland, Corporal Hechler reported that the 36th Ohio Volunteer Infantry had a new commander: Colonel W. G. Jones, who replaced Col. Andrews after the latter's return to the academic halls at Marietta College. In his letter of May 4, 1863, Corporal Hechler wrote his sister Kate in Marietta:

> There is a heavy fog here this morning, so that we can scarcely see a hundred yards.
>
> Colonel Jones had arrived here and taken command of the Regiment. Last Thursday we had muster and review at this post. It was the first time he had command of the regiment and he handled the regiment ably. He has already won the confidence of the men as an officer, and whether he will as a man remains to be seen. Just before the review the artillery fired a salute of ten guns, which caused considerable laughing among the boys on account of the stampede it caused among the darkeys.

General Joseph Hooker

Night before last three boats came up here loaded with provisions. Four of them had started but one stuck on the way. Some of our boys that were left behind in the hospital at Nashville when the regiment left there and came up now say that it was done purposely by her pilot, who they say talked treason on the way. Why is it the government employees Rebels in one of the most responsible positions in the service? Why not dismiss Rebel pilots as well as Generals and clerks? 1863 was the turning point of the Civil War, but the early summer had its disasters for the Union. Hooker took a terrible defeat at Chancellorsville. The boats started back this morning. A number from the 92nd Regiment were sent on them to Nashville hospitals.

Last week there were 16 deserters who came in from the Rebel army, mostly Kentuckians. Four brought their horses with them. They belonged to Morgan's command. They said there would be 500 in here before many days, but there is no sign of them coming yet.

There was also a report which came here by letter from Murfreesboro that Bragg had ordered his Army to fall back. The Tennesseans and Kentuckians refused, the result was a fight in which 800 were killed- 'a deserter's story.' One thing is certain, however, that is that they are in want of food, if not in actual starvation.

The copperheads at home do not discourage the Army, but make it more determined every day. They are utterly despised as mean and cowardly scoundrels, who are too big cowards to come out and fight for their country, and say that 'niggers' and such stuff are their pretense for not going. Their principles are not Southern, for they have none, nor are their sympathies there, for this is a quality they are strangers to. We have nothing to fear from them, only as far as they encourage their deluded brethren in the South, for all reports of talk from such persons go there and are magnified 10 times in the southern press.

No, they have not put me into any office other than corporal. But I had been detailed for picket duty the morning before the company went out. Pickets are relieved every morning, no matter who goes out, and if most of the force starts out at one time, the pickets are generally.

We have preaching here every Sunday and services once or twice during the week. Now and then we have a lecture from the Chaplain of the 11th. He is a good preacher and always has a good stock of humor on hand to sprinkle in his sermons. He generally has a large audience to preach to. He is, as he said, an impudent little fellow, prying into everybody's business, but this is what makes him liked here.

Brother John and I are well, hoping that God may speed the day when we may meet again, and peace be restored.

Your affectionate brother, George

THEN ON MAY 10, 1863, Corporal Hechler had this to write to his sister:

Well, Kate:

The letter you wrote to Brother John and me reached us and found us both well, the weather is rather warm today, but we have our tents raised off the ground, so there is plenty of fresh air in them, and they are now right comfortable. The last few nights have been cold for me. Had rain till Friday almost without stopping. The Cumberland River has risen and we now have plenty of clothing and supplies here.

Your invitation for dinner came too late for us to accept it, but I should like to take a good dinner with you, if you have plenty of lettuce and eggs. Pie plant pie would not taste bad, as we have not had any greens here, only one meal which we picked out tasted good, so we did not get any more. There are no garden vegetables to be had here now. We have had some potatoes lately, and today we are getting fresh beef. We have as much to eat as we want, such as it is, but we would like vegetables now.

Day after tomorrow a man with the name of Joe Smith, a spy, will be hanged here. He was caught by one of our men a few weeks ago, representing himself as a Rebel, when Joe told all he had ever done to injure the Yankees.

Last night company D of the 36th and some cavalry, afoot, went out on the other side of the river, and returned this morning bringing in one Colonel Smith, two or three other commissioned officers, and a few privates. There was a regiment of about 700 men camped within four or five hundred yards of the house the Colonel had taken up his quarters in. They followed and attacked our men, but as it was before daylight could not tell the number of our men. When fired on, they retreated helter-skelter, with the loss of two or three men, and several horses killed. None of our men hurt. They had been firing at us across the river for several days back, but have not hit anyone. They have not shown themselves yet today.

General Crook has been losing popularity among the men lately. He issued an order for making rails, some few have been made, but Captain Palmer is now under arrest for refusing to obey the order to detail men for the work; last night a big pile of rails was burned.

We are encamped on the plantation of McCollum. He has been a politician and made thousands of his money off the Government; spent a great deal in getting up Confederate troops, but has now taken the oath and of course, is a "good Union man" now, but the boys are not willing to build his fences, and if Crook

2ND LT. WILLIAM A. RHODES

will persist in it, he will find himself "outgeneraled" at last.

I have had a toothache for some time back. Today I went to the doctor to have the tooth pulled, but it was too decayed and broke off. I shall perhaps have the root dug up in a few days if the swelling goes down.

We have been off last week up to the first of March. I sent twenty dollars in an envelope by the Chaplain of the 92nd, directed to Hannah in care of Mr. Barber. I do not know whether it will be mailed at Marietta or not. I shall put one or two dollars in this letter.

Jones is our Colonel now. He is a good officer. Our lieutenants are Morrow and Rhodes, both good officers and liked by Company G.

The health of the troops is improving slowly at this Post. The health of our regiment is good and has been since we have been here.

Your brother, George

34. The Army of the Cumberland

Kennel Tents — Mud and Water — Pickets Captured

IN MID-MAY OF 1862, Lt. Augustus T. Ward, Co. G. 36th Ohio Volunteer Infantry, penned this note in his diary: "Rumor is that we are going back to West Virginia again as the Rebels are playing around about Parkersburg."

Down in Tennessee, the lads from Washington County, Ohio and Wood County, W. Va., were just moving out of their winter Sibley tents and into "shelter tents"—which they termed "Kennel tents."

On May 20, 1863, Corporal Hechler wrote:

> We drew shelter tents last Monday and the heat in them is almost intolerable. They are so low and flat. The sun seems to be coming down on them by some nearer way.
>
> There had been considerable excitement, but it has now nearly all disappeared. The general belief is that Hooker did not get much the best of the bargain with Lee. There is a rumor here that Crook, with the 11th and 36th Regiments, is going back to West Virginia. This would be welcome news to most of us here in the 36th.
>
> Today several families came in from across the river, but there is nothing done here now except some foraging. Last Saturday about 25 wagons went out after corn, with our regiment as guards. We got some bacon and a number of contrabands (Negro slaves) came in with us. Saturday night we camped about eight miles out, and Sunday morning Brother John and another one of the Company G boys found three hams in a fence corner. They

claimed the right of discovery, and the result was we had some good ham to eat. There was a Rebel cavalryman taken at a house where he was getting his dinner. He was all armed and he had a good horse. Today, fifty wagons were sent out again.

Two boats came up last night. They brought a large lot of southern goods and some of our deserters. Colonel Jones, our new regimental commander, is liked well in the regiment. He is trying to have company cooks, but has not succeeded yet. Company G cooked for themselves today, and Company A kicked the coffee kettle over this morning, and some went without food.

The news of Vallandigham's arrest was welcome here, and some wished that they had been there with the detachment. If he had fired, the number of shots would have been doubled, perhaps, as we are generally not very slow in returning any compliments or salute of that kind.

Brother John and I are both well.

Your loving brother, George

At the end of May, on May 31, 1863, Corporal Hechler wrote to his sister Kate in Marietta:

The weather today is pleasant and we have had showers for several days past, which cooled the air. We have shades built over our tents by setting forks into the ground, laying poles on them and covering the poles with brush. This makes them as comfortable as if they were standing in the shade of a tree. I have stood the hot weather well enough so far.

Night before last our regiment was out on an expedition and brought in about 17 prisoners and about 30 horses of Morgan's command without losing a man. Some of the Rebels shot only after our boys were almost upon them.

The health of the regiment is good. We have buried but one man since we have been here for three months. All the other regiments have lost more-the 92nd over seventy.

Your school and congregation in Harmar appears to have no lack of patriotism.

The $20 I sent I believe will total $100 now for safe-keeping. If you can find a safe place or person who wants to borrow the money, lend it. If not, put it in the bank so it will bear interest. I do not want any of the interest it may bear, but you may use it for yourself or devote it to some good purpose as you see fit during my absence. But I do not wish you to lend for a period of over a year.

I wish you would subscribe for the Marietta Register for me for six months.

We all have boards enough to sleep on, and have had for some time. General Crook's orders about Rebel property are generally not very effective. You may think from what I have written lately that the Regiment is discontented and inclined to mutiny, but that's not the case. All commands are obeyed promptly, and the rank and file knows them as well as any officer. Crook is still the choice of the 36th,

Your loving brother, George

Early in June, Corporal Hechler's outfit moved, as he wrote on June 11, 1863:

As you will see by this letter, we have left Carthage and come to near Murfreesboro. You would perhaps like to know what company we have got into. Well, as far as I can judge, they are very good as soldiers. We belong to the 3rd Brigade, 5th (Division), 14th Army Corps.

On the morning of the 3rd, orders were given to be ready to march at two o'clock in the afternoon, and soon the boats commenced crossing wagons over the Cumberland River. This is a slow business, and it was nearly two o'clock in the afternoon of the 4th when our regiment crossed. Ours was the last to cross the river, and the column marched about five miles more before we stopped to camp.

Sometime in the forenoon of the 4th, the Rebels captured three of our pickets. In the evening, Stokes' cavalry recaptured two of them and six Rebels to balance the account. Wednesday about eight o'clock a citizen was then under very suspicious circumstances. He was prepared to travel, and had once taken the oath of allegiance.

We passed through the little town of Alexandria about 11 o'clock, and there met the 17th Indiana. Alexandria is a beautiful little inland town. It has three churches in it, two of them with large steeples. Many of the inhabitants are loyal. Near this town I have seen the first ripe grain of 1863. It was a field of barley cut and shocked.

We marched to Liberty where we camped for the night. There was a force of our men there when we arrived. Wilder's Brigade was part of it. We had been short of meat for several days, and as we did not start the next morning and saw some fine hogs upon the hill, the men took an opportunity to draw some fresh pork.

A great part of Stokes' cavalry visited their friends and homes during the march. They have returned to Carthage again. Saturday afternoon, the 6th, we started again from Liberty, taking the Murfreesboro Road. Sunday evening we arrived in Murfreesboro. The country to here from Liberty is mostly level farms, the people Secesh, but few have left their property as far as I have seen. Many have large crops of wheat not ripening, and a considerable amount of corn growing. We are now camped on a field that had been planted in cotton last year, but now scarcely a fence is left for miles around and nothing has been planted.

I have not been in town yet. We are camped about two miles from town. Yesterday I saw four deserters from the Rebel Army come in. I was at the spring getting water when they came over to it, with their guards, and wanted a drink. Not one of them appeared to be over twenty. One of them had lived not over fifty yards from where he then stood.

I have no doubt that you see many different fashions and costumes represented at the Copperhead meeting in Marietta. But I suppose ignorance was the strongest represented of any one article there-bad whiskey excepted. But did you not wish you had been an artist, so that you could have drawn some of the oldest fashions for future use? For I have heard it said that fashions often return again. Perhaps some of them you saw there will return in a short time!

There was some murmuring about Vallandigham being sent south instead of punished. But the soldiers generally console themselves with the knowledge that 'Old Abe knows his business best', and are now satisfied about it.

I must, for my part, decline the invitation you sent me to

come to the picnic, as you did not state the time it was to come off. But if you had, I should most likely have some business or another sort to attend to on the plains of Tennessee or Mississippi. But I should like once more soon to be with friends at home, by the peaceful fireside, and see peace restored to our once prosperous country. I hope the time may soon come, but be it far or near, the Union shall again be restored as it was only freed from the curse of slavery.

Your loving brother, George

THERE WAS A STRANGE calm in the Army of the Cumberland in the early summer of 1863. It was clearly the calm before the storm of Chattanooga. Apprehensively, the Wood county and Washington County soldiers in Tennessee worried about reports that Jenkins, Morgan and other Rebel raiders were invading the Ohio River valley.

Cpl. Hechler wrote to his sister in Marietta on June 10, 1863.

Lee will hardly take his army into West Virginia as he could not support them there beyond the time the rations can be carried.

As the weather is pleasant today, I thought I would write a few lines to you. The sun is pretty warm, but there is nearly every day a cool breeze stirring, making shade quite comfortable. We have our camp fixed well now so that we don't have to be out, only when we choose to go, except morning and evening drills.

Our camp is on a hill, on which the last crop raised and harvested was cotton, and most of the land around here that I have seen yet has all the same appearance. The land is level, and the most of it very rich. There are some good springs about, but far between. There is no running water or stream nearer our camp than Stone River, and it is about two miles from our camp. The country about here is almost a wilderness. There is scarcely any fence left, only around gardens, houses, and the government has a few.

Last Sunday I got a pass to go and see Murfreesboro. It looks like a business place at present, to judge from the number of men seen there, but there is nothing allowed to be sold on Sunday, so all stores and sutler shops were closed. I passed on through the town to see the fortifications. These are the best constructed I have ever seen, and are still being strengthened. I only saw a small part of them, but they are well supplied with water and provisions and could stand a siege if only lightly garrisoned.

There is no sign in this Army yet, of any advance that I can see. Pickets are captured by both Armies occasionally. Yesterday got the news that the Rebels had taken Chambersburg (on the way to Gettysburg) and that Lee's whole Army is moving northward. There is not much excitement over it in our camp. It is generally thought that the Army of the Potomac, if a battle is fought, will gain one more victory, and the boys agree that if there will be much property destroyed it will cost less lives to conquer a peace, and may raise the North to the realities of war when they see the enemy at their doors. No doubt the Rebels mean to get all the supplies they can, but they will have precious little beyond what they eat while in the border states. But I hope Pittsburg, will be guarded to prevent them from entering it, for I have no doubt of the ability of their Cavalry to reach the place if they try.

The health of our Regiment is not as good as it was at Carthage, but none are dangerously sick. I am well, and so is Brother John. All that I can learn from this Army is favorable; it is now in good health, has confidence in itself and its commanders. You would hardly think there was a large Army camped here if you were in camp or traveling the roads. Everything seems to go on quietly, and there is no confusion.

Your loving brother, George

FROM CAMP BIG SPRING, Tennessee, Cpl. Hechler wrote to his sister in Marietta on July 15, 1863:

Dear Sister:

I received two letters from you since I wrote you, and I wish you to excuse my long delay, as I had no chance to write until a few days ago. Brother John and I are both well.

If the officers of the 36th Regiment bought any liquor and gave it to the men, I know nothing of it. At least, I never heard anything about it until I received your letter. I know they did not do it on the boat we were on, but did all they could to prevent the men from getting drunk. I am sorry to say a considerable number got drunk, getting their liquor mostly by going ashore at stopping places, but there was no disturbance aboard, any more than considerable hurrahing at one time, mingled with curses, and oaths, but the Major soon succeeded in getting them quiet. Had Col. Andrews been there, this might have taken a different turn.

I wish you would write in your next letter the name of the man who started the report about the officers. Col Andrews may be trying to sustain his supposed character, but it will not stand when the 36th Regiment gets back. He will certainly be branded a coward, if nothing more, I do not know whether all reports we have in camp have gone home to Marietta or not, I shall not write them now, as they may not all be true, but at Antietam when the men called on him to take command after Colonel Clarke fell, Andrews wanted to know where Captain Duval was, for , said he, "I am so fatigued!"

35. Marching Toward Dixie

Crook Idolized — Rumors of Rebels Deserting

GENERAL GEORGE CROOK, Indian fighter, tight-lipped leader of men, and the organizer of Hechler's 36th Ohio Volunteer Infantry Regiment, was idolized by his men. In Tennessee, General Crook was given command of the brigade in which Hechler served. But soon he was in line to be 2nd Cavalry Division Commander, and it was a sad day when the old troops gathered to listen to General Crook deliver his farewell address.

"General Turchin took command of our Brigade yesterday" wrote Corporal Hechler on July 31, 1863. "General Crook was ordered to take command of the 2nd Division of cavalry. I wish him much success. I have copied his farewell address and shall send the copy in this letter."

"Tears came to many eyes, as General Crook somewhat stiffly declared: 'Though separated from you, your actions and heroic deeds will always be watched and felt, with the pride of having once been your commander. My intimate association with the 36th Regiment, as its first commander, will pardon me for making any distinction. To them, by their actions upon the field, and in camp, by the spirit of those fallen, I am bound by an indissoluble tie.'"

But the genuine sentiments of the men of the 36th were not expressed until a day or two later. One of Hechler's close buddies reported: "General Crook came back to us today on some business. As he was leaving the quarters of Colonel Jones, the whole regiment was out looking at him, when, as he rode away, he raised his cap and waved it in farewell. As one man, the whole regiment gave a cheer, long and loud, that brought the old cap into the air repeatedly. Old hats were thrown aloft and when again returned to earth were stamped upon by their owners with as such zest as if it was a means of putting down the Rebellion. The men did not know how much they thought of him until they saw and felt that he was leaving them, perhaps, forever. He is a noble man militarily, and I much fear we shall never find another who will be to us what he has been."

FROM CAMP BIG SPRING in Tennessee, Cpl. Hechler wrote to his sister on July 31, 1863:

> I was wishing myself in Marietta after I heard of John Morgan getting into Ohio, just to see the people perform after getting excited. I think I could have enjoyed the fun right well. There was nothing wrong with putting up barricades with hay, but whoever gave the order to tear the bridge up when there was a turn in it certainly was out of his head at that time. If he thinks himself capable of holding an office in the military service. I wish he would go to Jeff Davis and Company to serve them if he is a Union man-he would do our government more good.
>
> I have heard from Harmar, but don't remember knowing Sharp, the Copperhead who was arrested in Marietta. Harmar would not lose much in heart. I will not deny but what Burch may have seen some of the officers buy liquor and give it to the men-as I have since writing my last letter heard, after inquiring of men that came to the boat with Colonel Andrews. But they all say no officer gave any of them enough to get drunk on, but did all they could to keep them sober, taking bottles from them and throwing them overboard.
>
> Big Spring has nearly gone dry, and it is rumored we will move tomorrow. I do not know where to, but it will be hardly over eight or ten miles. The roads are now dry, and nearly all the springs have stopped running, because there is no more water in the swamps. Wells afford plenty and good water, but one or two is not enough to supply a brigade.
>
> Your affectionate brother, George

Writing from camp near Jasper, Tenn., on August 22, 1863. Cpl. Hechler related:

> We have been marching toward Dixie slowly lately, and have nearly got to a little town called Jasper, 31 miles from Chattanooga. There have been plenty of peaches along the road, and we used them freely. We have all the corn we want to use and we nearly live on it, but it is all properly accounted for. I have never seen better corn than here in the valley of the Tennessee, or much more planted.
>
> The country around is not destroyed as much as at other places I have seen, but people seem to have suffered as much as anywhere. A good many are anxious to get away if the army goes. They say they don't want to stay and starve. They seem to look on our army, especially our mountaineers, the same as they would on plenty, and liberty to enjoy it. As far as we have come and I had a chance to find out, there are many Union people, and many others would be willing to have peace on any terms. They are tired of the war.
>
> We have not had any papers for several days, but had a rumor that Lee's army was deserting, some even fighting their way out. If this is the case, I think there is a prospect of peace soon-what we have all been wishing for some time past.
>
> We are ordered to fix up our camp today. Perhaps we will stay here a few days, as our trains have not come up yet. Some have no tools to work with. But you ask what do you have to fix up? Well, I will tell you. We stopped in an old field yesterday evening-here there are briars and other bushes to cut down, old cornstalks to pick up, and weeds to gather up and sweep off. Then the tents of each company will have to be put in one row and the streets shaded. Yesterday morning before we started we built a bunk to sleep on, but there is no chance for boards about here, so I suppose I will have to sleep on the ground as long as we stay here, and console myself thinking about the good bunk I am going to have to sleep on in the future.
>
> Brother John is well—and so am I.

Have any of the folks from home been to see you lately? Give my love to them, and keep a good share for yourself.

From your affectionate brother, George

Any officer who succeeded General Crook as commander of Hechler's "Kanawha Brigade" had a very tough assignment. So it was with the new brigade commander, General Turchin. The new general was described in this way by one of Hechler's buddies:

"General Turchin is now in command of our 'Kanawha Brigade'. He has a good reputation for fight. He is a corpulent, old Russian, and was in the service in Europe 19 years. Mrs. Turchin is with him. She is very fleshy, rides a white horse, and dressed in her riding habit she makes quite a soldierly appearance, attracting much attention. She pitches around among the troops as though she was their commander, looking as if to say: 'I am General Turchin's wife.'"

36. Brother John Missing

Chattanooga Captured — Terrible Butte

THE UNION VICTORIES at Gettysburg and Vicksburg in the summer of 1863 simultaneously dealt a stunning blow to the Confederate cause. The Rebel Army was reduced by over 50,000 men.

Meanwhile the Army of the Cumberland had pushed General Bragg back to Chattanooga. This freed all the country between the Ohio and Tennessee Rivers. Early in September, General Rosecrans, by a series of brilliant maneuvers, swung his Army of the Cumberland across the Tennessee River and captured Chattanooga. But then the bloody fighting started near this heart city of the South. It was one of the most stubbornly contested battles in American history, with two armies of about the same strength fighting with determined fury in the deep woods of north Georgia.

That was the Big Picture.

But to Corporal George Hechler, the bloody battle had a personal significance to him which tore at his heart-strings. Two years had passed since his younger brother John had failed to appear for breakfast at their little farm home on Harmar Hill. Brother John—the happy-go-lucky, devil-may-care, boisterous, bumptious and reckless youngster of the Hechler family-loved soldiering. More serious and steady, George Hechler looked after Brother John and helped him over many rough spots in the Army. But now came the bloody aftermath of Chattanooga, and to Brother John the start of a chain of events which eventually snuffed out his life.

From his camp in Georgia, near Chattanooga, George Hechler wrote on September 16, 1863:

Dear Sister,

I will try and write a few lines to you this forenoon, for the mail will start about noon.

This morning some mails came in, the first since six days. I got a Marietta Register of the 4th inst. This is the latest paper I have seen. There are, I think, later ones in camp.

The letter from you, directed to Brother John and myself, with a piece from Father in it, we got at Trenton about a week ago. I hope your hand will be well again by the time this reaches you. I am well, with the exception of diarrhea since yesterday morning, but feel considerably better now than early this morning. I think I can stop it by evening or rather it will stop of itself, as nothing is the best cure for it.

Brother John was well yesterday afternoon. He was on picket duty and has not come into camp yet this morning. They are not yet relieved. The pickets of both armies are not over 400 yards apart, but cannot see each other. Our regiment and part of the 11th was out yesterday and their pickets exchanged shots. No one was hurt on our side, and after finding out that they were there, we returned to camp. This morning at daylight, with arms, horse sacks and canteens, and all of us expected a battle would be fought today. After waiting about half an hour, we were dismissed again, so it seems put off again.

General Johnston is reported in command of the Rebel Army and if he brought his Corps together with Bragg's old Army and Buckner's from East Tennessee will make a hard fight if they fight at all in the strong position they occupy at present. Their troops have more confidence in Johnston than they had in Bragg. Chattanooga is in our possession, and the position of the Rebel Army is between 20 and 25 miles southeast from that place. They were busy all day yesterday blockading the road or fortifying.

The weather down here in Georgia is very hot in the daytime, but the nights are cool enough. As we have not had rain enough for six weeks to lay the dust and the ground is of a sandy nature, the dust is enough sometimes, almost to smother us,

General Joseph E. Johnston

together with the heat of the sun, but we have marched slowly.

The health of our regiment is as good, if not better, among the men present than ever before. Our company had one man on the sick list, but he marches with the company on a move. Company B had one man wounded in the arm last Saturday by a Rebel picket.

A breeze is stirring in the tree tops just now, and the leaves are falling fast. This reminds one that winter is close by.

There were a few shots fired just now in front.

Give my love to the folks at home.

Your affectionate brother, George

The first word of Brother John's fate came in Cpl. Hechler's letter to his sister on September 24, 1863 from Chattanooga:

Dear Sister:

I shall try and write a few lines to you today to let you know that I am yet well and un-injured, but it pains me to tell you that

Brother John is among the missing, and I very much fear killed or wounded. I have not heard anything from him since Sunday evening about 5 o'clock. The last I saw him was when the order to charge was given to our Brigade. We were surrounded, and our only way out was through the Rebel lines. We lost heavily there, as they pursued us a short distance.

Dear Sister, if it was the will of God that brother should give his life to the land of his adoption, and which I know he loved and still loves if he is alive, let us not murmur, but hope that he has gone to a better land where our beloved Mother long has dwelled. Let us pray that we may follow him. But I still have hope that he is injured and we shall soon see him again.

The battle, as you have doubtless heard before this, was terrible. We were outnumbered and surrounded, but hardly defeated as we forced the Rebels back and often scattered them, finally falling back to this place which we have been fortifying. The Rebels threw as few shots among us day before yesterday. Our boys captured the cannon they fired at us. Since then they have not disturbed us—only a little picket firing yesterday afternoon. Our artillery shelled the woods, and early this morning I was awakened by the boom of a gun. But all has been quiet with only the sound of orders from the fortifications since about seven this morning.

We are lying in reserve with a strong earthworks for protection from shot and shell in case of bombardment. Sherman's and McPherson's corps are ordered to join us, Rosecrans said yesterday evening. He said we have bored a small hole into the Confederacy, and with the help of God, when they come we will make it larger. Rosecrans looks well and seems in good spirits.

The Army is still confident of success. All Rebel prisoners admit that their cause will not succeed, but think they can carry on the war several years longer. May God speedily bring them to reason that bloodshed and desolation may soon cease.

Colonel Jones, our regimental commander, died Sunday morning. Major Adney was wounded. He came up to see us Tuesday on horseback, but it caused him much pain in his hip.

Your affectionate brother, George

37. Battle of Chickamauga

Looking For John — Desperate Test Attack on the Pontoons

General George H. Thomas became known in history as "The Rock of Chickamauga." This noble Virginian who fought for the Union Army, a determined fighter and great tactician saved the day after a desperate series of small-unit struggles in the thickets of Tennessee. But it took more than the Rock of Chickamauga to save thousands of the Union and the Confederacy, wiped out on the field of battle. Included among the missing was Private John Hechler, who had run away from his Marietta home to enlist, and was the brother of Corporal George Hechler.

Cpl. George Hechler wrote to his sister Kate in Marietta on October 5, 1863.

> Our wounded have now nearly all come in, but I have not been able to find John among them. One man from our company that was wounded just as our regiment started toward the Rebel line Sunday evening, said he stopped with Brother John, took out his tent and stayed a little while, went away, and after a few minutes came back again. Then he stopped till the Rebels came in plain view from the opposite side. It was then impossible for any man to get away without going through their lines and I hope that Brother John is only a prisoner.
>
> You have no doubt heard about the fight more than I can tell you, but I will tell you how I fared from Thursday before the fight. That day we were out on a reconnaissance all day. We started just after we had commenced eating breakfast, came in at

General George H. Thomas

dark, and I was detailed for regimental guard duty. I didn't sleep much that night. Friday forenoon we moved about a mile, and after having tents up we were ordered to be ready to march at a moment's warning. So the knapsacks were packed again, but we did not start till after dark, then had an all-night march of six to eight miles.

Saturday morning, after we stopped, there was no water but one well nearer than Crawfish Springs. It was nearly two miles back or to the right as our line lay. I went to the spring after water and had hardly finished eating my breakfast as the order came to fall in. The night before had been cold and every fence along the roadside had been set on fire by the troops to warm by and march by its light. We were soon formed in a line; one brigade was fighting ahead of us. They sent for reinforcements, and four companies from our regiment were sent, but the enemy retreated before they got near enough to do anything. We then marched and counter-marched nearly two hours before we took a position. Our regiment lay in reserve for the brigade, following up the line till about three o'clock, when heavy firing to the right put a stop to our advance. It soon rolled back to our rear. We started double quick, and soon saw the Rebels close after the 21st Indiana battery, without any infantry to oppose them. Colonel Jones led our regiment between them and the guns, and there he received his fatal wound. Major Adney was also wounded. The fighting for a few minutes was the hardest our regiment has done yet. But the fear of our bayonets put them to flight. A little while afterward we were relieved for the night.

I had not eaten anything since morning, and only enough for one meal was in my horse-sack, so I drank about a half pint of coffee and ate a few bites, then laid down but could not sleep much. Sunday morning I shared my horse-sack, or rather the contents of it, with one of the boys who had nothing. Now it had gotten so late we began to think the Rebels would not disturb us, but we were disappointed. The fight commenced nearly all at once, along the whole line, the Rebel skirmishers telling ours that they were now fighting Eastern troops and not General Bragg—and some of ours asking if they remembered South Mountain. Our position was behind breastworks made of old logs, so that we were safe from bullets as long as we were behind it. The Rebels made several shows of attack, but came no nearer than 200 yards in front of our regiment.

First our left gave way, but checked them again. The right-composed of Crittenden's and McCook's Corps, or most of them-was rolled back and soon scattered so that the enemy's lines formed nearly a triangle around us, our brigade lying in the angle, which we soon found out by the bullets of their sharpshooters, but they did us little damage.

About five in the evening we were ordered to fall in. We had been lying down. After going about half a mile, we saw several Generals, among them Thomas ("The Rock of Chickamauga"), together; he formed our brigade and told Turchin, our brigade commander, which way to go. The Rebels were forming a line in our front, and without command-or if any was given few heard it—the whole brigade started with a yell, but few stopped to fire. The Rebels followed suit, and soon the greybacks were seen in every direction, running their best, but we captured over 300 of them-one General among the number.

There was where Brother John stopped. All the time we were going about a mile we were exposed to fire from the right flank of the line of infantry and one or two batteries. Our whole loss there of the brigade would not amount to 100 men, some of them we know were not hurt but only taken prisoner. General Reynolds and about 150 men chased a detachment of Rebel cavalry over two miles. They kept up a running fight at long range.

We stopped near one of our hospitals and Colonel Lane, of the 11th Ohio, told us that under no circumstances would it do to fire there, but we would have to surrender if we could not get away. This was unpleasant, but we soon found out that the way was open to Granger's men, and we soon afterward found the brigade. That night we moved back to Bassville and I got a few hours sleep, after drinking some coffee. Next morning we drew some rations, and Monday night after some skirmishing the whole army fell back to Chattanooga, where we are now. Part of our men have been to work on the trenches night and day since we came here, and between the Rebels and our work this is becoming a strong position. (The Rebels had fortified earlier.)

Last Saturday this whole army was put on half rations, and every horse that can possibly be spared had been sent off. Today there has been considerable artillery firing, and some of the Rebel cannonballs have come in about 150 yards from my tent. Our division has no duty to do in the trenches. Picket is our duty when in camp. We are away in the rear of the works. It is rumored that four corps are coming to reinforce us and that about 600 wagons had been destroyed by the confederate cavalry a few days ago.

The Tennessee River has risen considerable in the last few days, so that it will be impossible to ford it anywhere near here. The Army is yet in good spirits in spite of their heavy loss. Our corps lost one half, or about 13,000, but many of them were straggling when the report was made out, and have since joined their commands. Several regiments that I know of have added over 100 each.

Hoping this will find you well, I bid you goodbye for a little while only, and hope to remain,

Your affectionate brother, George

WHEN THE NEW REGIMENTAL commander of the 36th Ohio Regiment, high-spirited Colonel William G. Jones, led his regiment into battle at Chickamauga, one of the first things he saw was a flurry of scattering and fleeing bluecoats of the Union Army. Colonel Jones drew his sword, which one of his men said "rang like an anvil" against his scabbard, and shouted; "We'll let them know this is a regiment that can't run!"

Colonel Jones knew that Chickamauga would be a desperate test for the regiment recruited in the Marietta-Parkersburg area. He noted in his pocket diary: "Off to the left; merciful Father, have mercy on me and my regiment, and protect us from injury and death." But death came quickly to the regimental commander, and scores of the regiments bravest, including Pvt. John Hechler were killed or captured at Chickamauga.

After the battle, Cpl. George Hechler wrote from Chattanooga on October 11, 1863:

> Our regiment again talks of going back to West Virginia with General Crook. I hope we will. He has paid us a short visit since the fight. Some of the boys asked him about the report of his being ordered here, and he said that he had received a letter from Governor Boreman (of Parkersburg) about it that day, but did not want to go unless he could get the 36th with him.
>
> I have not heard anything more from Brother John since I wrote my last letter. The Rebels have not troubled us any since. There is some rumor that they are falling back and that their shelling that day was caused by a fight among themselves. The Tennesseans were trying to get away. Report says that several thousand were killed and wounded, and we have continually rumors in camp of hundreds that have come in and given themselves up. I cannot say how true all these reports are, as I have not seen any of the hundreds.
>
> But last Wednesday when our regiment was on picket I saw one come in. He was well-dressed and his clothes were clean, but he said he had only been up from the hospital two days. Our pickets are in sight and in some places in easy gunshot of each other, but they

scarcely ever shoot. We were exchanging papers that day this Rebel soldier came out to exchange, but after he had our paper he, instead of going clean back, went to a low place and came into our lines. He claimed to be a picket in the 2nd Tennessee. Among the Rebel news was that all the Yankees had left the south bank of the Tennessee River, but their tune seems to be despondent about their late victory. At Chattanooga they admit a loss of from 25 to 35,000 and say there will be nothing gained unless they get Chattanooga itself. But before they can get this place now it would be necessary for them to fight harder than they did in the last battle, and I do not think they are capable of doing that.

We have got some new clothes now and full rations again, so that we are tolerably comfortable. The nights are cold but we have our shelter tents boarded up at each end now, and can sleep tolerably warm under two blankets.

Our division has been broken up. General Reynolds was assigned to some fortification on General Rosecrans' staff . . . the 21st Indiana battery has been with our brigade since we went to Nashville, and its ranks have been filled by detailed men from the different regiments in the brigade. All of them were ordered back yesterday evening. It has now only men enough to work four guns, but they moved camp last night. I do not know where we belong now, what division or corps.

I am yet well, and hope these few lines will find you well,

Your affectionate brother, George

A FEW DAYS LATER on October 20, 1863, Cpl. Hechler wrote gloomily: "We have almost given up hopes again of going to West Virginia." He was also pained to report: "I have not heard nothing more of Brother John."

"There is nothing new going on here," Cpl. Hechler reported to his sister Kate in Marietta.

The Rebels have left us alone since I wrote the last time. The weather has been very bad, and it rained several days almost without stopping. Some of the Rebels, though not many, came into our lines. One of them said when asked what he came for, he thought he had been out long enough and wanted to come into the dry. The most of the deserters are Tennesseans, but some Mississippians of Longstreet's corps have come in lately.

Every deserter encourages our army to some extent, as many afterward join them and many such are weakening the Rebel Army faster than many at home would be willing to believe.

During the rise in the river, General Bragg sent down trees and rafts to destroy our pontoons. They had to be opened once, but he did us much more good than harm, for we need wood for fortifications. There is a small steamboat here in the river. With it most of the timber was caught and towed ashore. Some of it is now where Bragg would least want it would he make an attack on this place.

The Rebels claim to have 300 pieces of artillery in front of Chattanooga, and are promising us a warm time of it, here shortly. They have almost left Lookout Mountain, or else doing without fire there, but they have perhaps learned by experience that it won't pay to waste ammunition from there.

The Army has been reorganized and are moving camp today. Our regiment and the 89th are on picket today, so we will perhaps have to move tomorrow. The reason I am not on picket today as I was on regimental guard last night.

We heard that Ohio has given Brough 72,000 majority at home (in election for Governor.) The soldiers' vote is almost a clear majority. The 36th polled 396 voted for Brough, and 4 for Vallandigham, Company C's vote is not included in this, as they are still away guarding trains between here and Stevenson. The 92nd has one Vallandigham, the 11th none, the 89th twenty-seven, and I think the whole Army will go about the same. Many are glad that there are some votes for Vallandigham for they say it will show that the election was held fairly and not interfered with by the officers, as no doubt the cry will be among the Copperheads—as it is now.

Yesterday and today the weather has been clear and warm, but the nights are cool and generally foggy.

Here's hoping that this war will soon be over, and we be permitted to be together again, I remain,

Your affectionate brother, George

38. The Fight for Tennessee

Fond of Flowers — Wilds of Tennessee
Election of Governor

ATOP HARMAR HILL near Marietta, a young woman named Kate Hechler spent a considerable amount of time between her heavy farm chores in writing letters to her two brothers in the Union Army. With a rare sensitivity, Kate Hechler related those events of home and hearth which gave her brothers the feeling of what they were fighting to preserve. She told about developments on the Hechler farm, goings-on at the church, local gossip, romances which were developing, and how things were doing over in Parkersburg, Williamstown and in the Wirt and Ritchie County oil fields.

Knowing that her brother George was extremely fond of flowers, Kate Hechler would frequently press and send him samples of the beauty of the Ohio Valley in her letters.

"Kate, I wish you would continue putting flowers into your letters as long as you have them," wrote Cpl. George Hechler from Chattanooga. " I love flowers, especially now that fall has stripped the trees of their leaves and everything looks bare and desolate about here. They remind me of all the beautiful times I have had while working on the farm. Still, I do not regret that I have enlisted, but if I live through this war I would want to probably go at farming again."

Nonetheless, there was a deep shadow still across George Hechler as he prepared for the winter in Tennessee. Brother John, still missing after the bloody battle of Chickamauga, was unheard from. "Have you ever seen Brother John's name in any Cincinnati paper in a list reported by the Rebels as prisoners without being injured? I have heard it was there, but never could find it myself," wrote Cpl. Hechler to his sister. Frantically, he tried to piece together news from Libby Prison, the Confederate prison in Richmond.

"I have heard from several of the boys in Richmond," Cpl. Hechler wrote, "James Bliss has written to Captain Palmer that he was there in Richmond uninjured. Another member of Company G has written home from there that they had good, comfortable quarters. He said nothing about the food, I have not heard Brother John's name mentioned yet by anybody that is at Libby Prison in Richmond, but I still hope for the best. A prisoner's lot is now in the hands of the Rebels. It is certainly not a desirable one from all accounts we receive, but if John was not robbed of his money when taken, he can, by a little economy, make out to live without suffering for several months, unless the prisoners there now have not as much liberty as they had a year ago."

MEANWHILE, THE FIGHTING went on in the wilds of Tennessee. On November 7, 1863, Cpl. Hechler wrote his sister:

> I received your letter dated the 11th of last month about two weeks ago, I should have written sooner, but had no chance as a plan had been formed to capture the lower portion of Lookout Valley and put up a pontoon bridge, so as to cooperate with Hooker who was coming from Bridgeport, on the South side of the Tennessee River, Hagen's and Turchin's brigade were ordered to go. Our brigade crossed the river after dark and marched across a neck of land, then stopped till nearly daylight. The river is very crooked here. It is nine miles around by the river and only about two across to where the bridge was put up. The other brigade started after midnight on the pontoon boats and floated past Lookout Mountain. The Rebels along the bank, after some argument and voting several among their company 'fools', came to the conclusion that there was nothing but drift floating down and they need not disturb it. As soon as the boats reached the

place where they were to land, the Rebels were so taken by surprise that they did not fight much, and our boys soon had possession of the bluffs near the river.

After our brigade crossed, the bridge was put up, the Rebels keeping on firing from artillery until nearly noon. We worked hard putting up breastworks till nearly eight when we had them finished. There was no one hurt by shells that I have heard of. Our loss was seven or eight killed and about fifteen wounded. The Rebels left eight or 10 dead on the field.

In the evening, the boys looked for signs from Hooker, but nothing could be seen. Next morning Wednesday, the Rebels shelled our works from the top of the mountain till about two in the afternoon, when they shifted their pieces and then shelled into Lookout Valley. We were then satisfied that Old Joe (Hooker), as he is generally called in the Army, was near. He had not lost any of his fighting reputation since coming here either, for the first night after being there two of his regiments attacked and routed a division of Rebels, driving them from behind breastworks off a hill. They lost about 175 killed and wounded, but killed and wounded more Rebels and captured about 200 besides. It was about time we got the river or we would have to leave this place.

While we stopped there, we had nothing to eat but parched corn. After staying there nine days without tents we returned to camp. We have a prospect now of getting plenty of rations soon, as there are several boats running within a few miles of here, carrying supplies from Bridgeport, but for the last three weeks we have scarcely had half rations. I am well, however, and have not been suffering yet for lack of something to eat, as you would think if you could see my face. I gained eight pounds of weight from the time we started to cross Lookout Mountain till we came to Chattanooga just after the battle, and I suspect would weigh still heavier now.

The Rebels have long-range guns now on the mountain and fire every day. Now and then a shell or shot falls in or near town without much harm. I remain

Your affectionate brother, George

IN HIS NEXT LETTER from Chattanooga on November 14, 1863, Cpl. Hechler commented on the election results in the race for Governor of Ohio:

> How the soldiers are satisfied with the results of the election you can find best in the returns of the soldier votes. To the certain sum soldiers were paid by officers to vote for Brough, it must have been large, but when the ones would be looked after who voted for Vallandigham in the 36th, I think their votes might be bought cheaper. A quart of whiskey might have a good deal of influence with any of them. But if they that raise the cry about money paid for votes had the courage to come out and tell us, we could soon pay them off in the kind of coin we generally do the Rebels. Perhaps they would soon be satisfied.
>
> We think out here that the election has done as much to discourage the Rebels as a defeat in the field, for before the election prisoners would speak confidently of Vallandigham's election and the divisions it would cause at home. They thought they could hold out that long. Scarcely any of them had hopes of ever gaining what they term their independence, liberty or rights from a united North. We had to acknowledge that there was a strong peace party in the North. Now we can tell them we are united as even Governor Seymour, who was elected by a Copperhead majority, is denounced as an Abolitionist by that same party for the support he is giving the Administration.
>
> Last night we were out on picket. The Rebels shot three shots yesterday afternoon from Lookout Mountain over our heads. They have wounded but one man that I have heard of for over one month back by their cannonading from there, and they are doing more or less of it every day.
>
> Today our regiment is being paid off. Company G will be in a few minutes. I shall try and send some money, but do not know yet how much. I will put two dollars in this.
>
> Please renew my subscription for the Register again for six

months. By it I can always find out what is going on about Marietta. If you read Captain Palmer's letter in the paper of the 6th of this month, it will give you an idea of our position here. The foot of Lookout Mountain would be about two miles further down the river from where he places our right.

Your loving brother, George

39. The Battle of Missionary Ridge

Furlough Requests — Decisive Victory

WINTER WAS SETTING IN at Chattanooga in 1863. A rugged, leonine Union Army commander named General George H. Thomas, known to his men as "The Rock of Chickamauga," was approached one day by a young Ohio Valley soldier who wanted a furlough.

"I ain't seen my old woman, General, for four months."

The burly general gruffly replied: "And I have not seen mine for two years; if a general can practice restraint, surely a private can too."

"Don't know about that, General," said the soldier. "You see, me and my wife ain't made that way."

The Army of the Cumberland was licking its wounds after the disaster of Chickamauga. It would not be too long before the new battle of Missionary Ridge at the end of November, 1863.

"I will try this foggy morning and write a few lines to you, as we have no drill today," wrote Corporal Hechler to his sister, Kate in Marietta on November 18, 1863.

> Yesterday we had four hours of drill, two in the forenoon at bayonet drill; and brigade and regimental drill in the afternoon.
>
> I was working with the military police—not working but guarding two men who were in the workhouse while they were working. Today, a good part of the regiment was detailed to work at a fort. Heavy artillery has been brought up lately and the field pieces are taken out, rebuilt and heavy guns mounted at the fort as fast as possible.
>
> General Bragg has not made any change that I can see in our

front. Yesterday morning there was heavy fighting for about an hour, a few miles up the river. The report is that Sherman's troops crossed there and captured a number of prisoners, at the same time driving Bragg's right from the river so that the Army could march around his defensive works on Missionary Ridge. I do not know how true this is, for I was not there to see.

I have not heard anything of Brother John yet, but still hope for the best.

I have paid fifty dollars to the State Agent to be paid to you. I shall send the receipt in this letter. When the money is paid to the county treasurer you will find out, then you can either send after it by someone or get it yourself. You may lend the money to father if he wants to borrow, and take a note from him for the amount, either in your or my name.

None of our deserters have been paid yet since they came back. Part of them are in the guardhouse and will have their trial soon. One was brought back last week. I would not want to be in their places for I believe some of them will be severely punished. Last Friday, two deserters were shot. I don't know whether there were other charges against them or not.

Your affectionate brother, George.

IN HIS NEXT LETTER on November 30, 1863, Corporal Hechler described the battle of Missionary Ridge and Lookout Mountain:

Dear Sister:

I received your letter dated November 20th on the 27th. We were then about eighteen or twenty miles from Chattanooga, where we had gone after the battle. You have no doubt heard before this time there has been another hard battle fought here, and with the help of God a great and almost decisive victory won. I do not think there are as many killed and wounded as at Chickamauga, but if reports are true General Bragg's army is about to be among the things that have been. Over 100 pieces of cannon and 30,000 prisoners are reported captured. One week ago today, Monday, we started out of camp and came back last night after dark.

Although we did not go very far Monday afternoon, we went about fifty yards outside our pickets. Our company was out as skirmishers and the Rebel outpost nearest us fired their guns up in the air and ran away. That was all the firing done on our part of the line. There was some fighting on the left of our line that day. After dark, we lay down but before I was asleep the pickets near us amused themselves with a little harmless shooting for a few minutes. Shortly afterward, one gun was fired on our front, and a man heard to say: 'I am shot.' He was a Rebel soldier, and had gotten tired and started to come into our lines. One of their pickets shot him. This proves how much risk they run in deserting, and still some are daily coming in.

Tuesday, forenoon fighting commenced on Lookout Mountain. Many of our men looking in that direction said-it seemed before they stopped to think: 'Boys, we have them out-generaled.' This was the first time I heard it said by any of the soldiers at the commencing of a battle. The firing came nearer very fast, and we anxiously watched the Mountain. Our men attacked them on the opposite side, and they had to come around the point on our right or separate for a long distance from the rest of the Rebel Army. We soon saw a flag-we first supposed it was Rebel, as we had not seen anyone pass around yet. But the dark blue line moving around with it soon told plainly enough that they were our men. We were too far away to see the scattering greybacks with the naked eye, on account of the color of their uniforms. Several cheers were given on our right and taken up along the line in front of Chattanooga.

Our brigade commander, General Turchin, wanted to go there with his brigade and a battery, for he said he thought they could do much good. He did not get leave to go, as another general had already been ordered to go. We had nothing more to do till Wednesday afternoon when the old Army of the Cumberland and nearly all of Hooker's and Sherman's troops made an attack on Missionary Ridge, after a short fight drove the Rebels from nearly every point of it-that is, all that could get away and felt like doing so. You may imagine the noise of guns and bursting shells of nearly all sizes, and some of our heavy guns mingled their roar with those of the Rebels.

A short time after we had gained Missionary Ridge, a loud cheer rolled from right toward left of our line, and we soon saw General Grant. He stopped right before us, as the officers were trying to form the regiment. He paid no attention to the cheers given. There was still fighting going on farther to the left, and his whole mind seemed to be on it. He seemed impatient sitting on his horse; it seemed equally so, and made several motions as if to start. One of the General's staff said: 'General, you had better not go out there too far.' Soon after that he turned his horse and galloped back.

After night we came back to the foot of the hill where the Rebel shanties made good camp fire during the night. Thursday morning, we went up the hill again. Each man had gotten 100 rounds of cartridges, and they told us four day's rations. This looked like a fight or a foot-race. About 10 o'clock we started east and after a few hours returned to the hill again. At noon while we were out sitting down on the hillside, we heard the boom of a cannon at Chattanooga. After the second cannon was fired, some asked: "What does it mean?"

Others answered: "It is a salute, this is Thanksgiving Day, and it is a national salute." I can tell you what I had for Thanksgiving Dinner that day-perhaps you would like to know. I had some crackers, a little sugar and a slice of raw bacon to eat and some water to drink, and if you would have called around you might have had a piece of raw bacon for your dinner.

About twenty prisoners passed our regiment that day, from Thursday till we came back yesterday morning nothing of any importance happened to our division. We saw the marks of a hasty flight by the Rebels along the road-such as cannon, caissons, wagons, small arms, and large quantities of ammunition, besides a little corn, rice and flour scattered along the road. They made a halt near Ringgold, but were soon driven from there. We lost about 300 killed and wounded. Our company had three wounded, none of them dangerously, and one missing during this last night. All three of the wounded are up and about, and two of them will do duty again in about a week. I am yet well and unhurt.

There is a mixed account of what I know of the last battle. I do not know whether you can find any sense in it, or that you can have any idea of what it means. I do not care about knowing what Colonel Andrews has said. Perhaps you will not blame the 36th much for trying to get rid of him, for if his character is little, his capability as a commander is smaller still.

I must close now, for the fire is getting low, the day is cold, and we have but little wood. Besides, if we do have a little fire the fireplace smokes at the wrong end today, on account of the cold wind, I suppose.

I must tell you yet that a large part of the Army has left for some other part of the country or Confederacy.

Write soon to
your affectionate brother, George

40. Horrifying Sights

Unhappy Christmas — Promotion Discussion — Gettysburg

As the final days and minutes of 1863 ticked away, the members of the 36th Ohio Volunteer Infantry Regiment looked forward to their reenlistment furloughs when they could return to Washington County, Ohio and the Parkersburg area to see their loved ones again. February, 1864 was the month set aside for furloughs if all went well on the war-front.

For Corporal George Hechler, the onset of the Christmas season was not a happy one. He still had heard no direct news from Brother John, missing in the bloody battle of Chickamauga. A small ray of hope came in December and Corporal Hechler wrote his sister on December 4, 1863:

> Brother John's name has been mentioned in a letter from Richmond as being there, as one of our company told me yesterday his father had written to him. I hope the Rebels do not treat all the prisoners as they have some they sent into our lines lately, but hope the Government will not be forced into an exchange of prisoners by them, for the power of the rebellion is now broken and no advantage should be given them.
>
> Perhaps you have received the letter I sent you a few days ago about the fight. The number of captured I wrote about was only rumor and the papers will have the true account but by it you will see what wild stories we generally have circulating in camp, as that is a very good specimen of them. I have learned to make considerable allowance. Some of the troops that were reported

> gone have again turned up near this place. I think the most of this army will stop near here for some time, at least till it can be supplied with clothing and rations-something we have not had for several months, though the health of the army could not be expected to be any better.
>
> The war may not be more than half over, but still there are sure signs of brighter days coming. One is the number of deserters coming into our lines. We cannot starve them out, unless there is less corn farther south. In northern Georgia there has been a large amount of corn raised and I believe that there is enough within the Rebel lines to keep all that are there.
>
> You will notice that Sherman and Hooker both were engaged. Sherman was repulsed, but after Bragg commenced retreating he made up his loss. Prisoners said, after we captured them on Missionary Ridge, you have whipped our left, and we have yours. We did not believe it then, but know it now.
>
> The fighting was hard while it lasted. The Rebels never once thought that the Yankees would be fools enough to storm their position from the front, and they expected to repulse any attack made on them there.

Now, in a subtle change of pace, Corporal Hechler slyly remarked to his sister Kate In Marietta:

> You asked me if I did not think you had better think about getting married. I think it is nearly time to let thinking alone and be doing—though I should like very much to be present at your wedding. Won't you invite me?
>
> Your loving brother, George

IN HIS NEXT LETTER from Chattanooga, dated December 14, 1863, Corporal Hechler modestly discounted any rumors that he might merit a further promotion. "The many flattering reports you say you heard about me, you had perhaps better take with some allowance. As to my present position proving a stepping stone, I sincerely hope it will not for I would much rather see the war closed soon than take any position of trust or profit in the service which, by the way, there is not much danger of either should I continue in the service another term."

Corporal Hechler was horrified with the battlefield scene as he returned to the field where so much blood had been shed at Chickamauga. "We have been on the battleground of Chickamauga lately," he wrote. "I did not see any bodies with heads cut off, but do not wish to see another such sight. Most of our men were buried on top of the ground by having a few shovels full of dirt thrown over them. Heads and feet of most are now washed out. A few of both armies were never buried at all. No doubt they were not found on account of the leaves. Most of the Rebel dead were decently buried and marked, and there are far more marked than unmarked graves. The body of our regimental commander, Colonel Jones and several other officers were taken up and brought in. The 9th and the 36th Ohio and 10th Indiana were all the troops out. General Grant, and many others I don't know, rode over and inspected the battleground. Howard, the one-armed man was there." (General O. O. Howard, whose right arm had been shattered in the Seven Day's Battles of 1862, had ridden up to observe when he saw General Phil Kearney's left arm was shot off: "Hereafter we buy our gloves together.")

> Your letter dated 27th of last month I received a few days ago. What little there will be left out of the two dollars after subscribing for The Marietta Register you may do what you please with. The 50 you may deposit in the bank or invest them in government securities as you think best.
>
> I have not heard anything from Brother John yet since I wrote you last. Martin Schwartz was sent to the hospital a few days ago. He was reduced nearly to a skeleton by the chronic diarrhea.
>
> I am well yet. My horse sack sometimes, though, takes a bad disease and the consequence generally is that I feel disagreeable for about a half a day. But we hope to see some trains come in over the railroad around the foot of Lookout Mountain near the river, then we can prevent such diseases.

I do not know how near the road is to being rebuilt. There are not many troops in or about town. A few still work on the fortifications.

Much love from

Your affectionate brother, George

ONLY A FEW DAYS before Corporal Hechler returned to the battlefield at Chickamauga, a printed circular had arrived on President Abraham Lincoln's desk at the White House, inviting him to the battlefield of Gettysburg to dedicate a cemetery. President Lincoln felt deeply that in the helpless onrush of the Civil War, too many brave men had lain neglected in the open fields just as Corporal Hechler had seen them at Chickamauga. Although not invited personally, President Lincoln considered the form invitation to Gettysburg important enough to accept. Those in charge of the ceremonies, having invited the great orator Edward Everett to deliver the main oration, were amazed that President Lincoln had accepted, and one of them wrote: "The question was raised as to his ability to speak upon such a grave and solemn occasion. With his important duties and responsibilities, he could not possibly have the leisure to prepare an address."

This week we celebrate the birthday of the man who arose at Gettysburg, and in few brief sentences delivered the address which best expressed the meaning of democracy, freedom and the American dream.

41. Return to Marietta

Rumors of Peace — Furlough
Stirring Words — Growing City — Back to the Front

IN THE FINAL TWO LETTERS that Corporal Hechler wrote before returning to Parkersburg and Marietta for his re-enlistment furlough, he again expressed deep concern over the possible fate of his Brother John, missing in action at the bloody battle of Chickamauga. On December 20, 1863, Corporal Hechler wrote from Chattanooga to his sister in Marietta:

"Albert Foster told me his Father wrote to him that James Oliver mentioned Brother John's name as being in Richmond. But Oliver had written a letter to Captain Palmer from Libby Prison and did not mention John as one of them. You want me to tell you what I think about it? I scarcely know what to say, dear sister, I hope and fear, but lately I have strong hopes of again seeing him with us before long, or at least before this regiment leaves the service, which should be in eight months or less."

Meanwhile, there was still talk circulating around the campfires of the Union Army about the possibility that the Rebels might sue for peace. Corporal Hechler wrote to his sister Kate in the same letter:

> There is a report current in camp of Peace Commissioners having arrived in Washington from Richmond, and that the Rebel Government has asked for an armistice of ninety days. The first is not generally believed, and if the second were put to a vote in the Army

the Rebels would stand about as good a chance getting it as Vallandigham did Governor, much as we desire rest. The Army knows what advantage can be given in three months by the South. The people there are now discouraged and in dread of our cavalry. They were, at the commencement of the war, enthusiastic for it. But they have suffered by it, and hatred against the Yankees took its place. Now many of them are being un-deceived, and hail the Northern armies as their deliverers. Of course, some of them are still rebellious, but they have given up nearly all hope of ever gaining what they call their rights. We may have to fight some hard battle yet, if not settled this winter, for there is plenty of corn and considerable beef yet in the Confederacy-what the Rebel Army was said to have lived on for months, according to prisoners, and they all looked hearty and well. But by far the most of them will prefer to be slaves of the North as Southern papers call it, than freemen of the Jeff Davis Con-thieveracy. Then why should I doubt about the issue of this war?

The weather this Sunday afternoon is clear and would be pleasant if a little warmer. Last night I think was the coldest we have had here this winter. We have not seen any snow yet since we came to Chattanooga, although we have had some cold and very disagreeable rains.

Yesterday the 15th Army corps passed here on their way down or back somewhere. Some of them appeared to think that their next campaign will be against Mobile.

I received the stamps you sent all safe. You may deposit the money in the bank; it will suit me as well as any way.

The story about the Rebels mutilating the bodies of our dead at Chickamauga seem to be true. I have not seen any myself, as I wrote in my last letter, but some of our men that I would believe and trust say they saw a few heads and skulls on stumps and logs, none on poles that I can hear of.

I have seen the notice of the Fair, for the benefit of sick and wounded soldiers, in the Marietta Register. I hope it was a good success.

Christmas will soon be around. We had hoped there would be a chance to buy something in the city by that time, but our prospects have nearly got blue or something else, and the railroad is not finished yet and all other transportation used for rations.

No sutlers are allowed here now unless they have been ordered up lately.

I am not so very anxious about having you to marry. I certainly should not like to have a Copperhead for a brother-in-law. I wrote the way I did thinking but of your age at the time, and you will certainly not say I was wrong in that respect.

I received the Marietta Register of the 11th this morning, and read about the disobedience of orders by the soldiers in the Battle of Mission Ridge. But General Grant, nor any other man, or power on earth would have held the Army of the Cumberland at the Rebel works near the foot of the hill. They no doubt had anticipated such a move and had accurate range of the works, besides being within what we call graping distance, but by going forward they would lose range. So most of the men concluded that forward was the safest way. They thought perhaps the Rebels would take a scare, which they did, but they stood longer in our front than I could have believed possible. This is the first time they waited for our regiment to get so near that the opposing rifles' flame reached the men that fired them. I did not get up to that place, my breath having given out part of the way up the hill, and some of the officers tried to form the regiment in our place for fear that the Rebels would turn on us.

The Rebels blame their soldiers for losing this battle. As soldiers they are not to blame, for even Longstreet's boasted troops, McLaw's Brigade-which they consider the best in the Rebel service—never fought as stubbornly as they did at Chickamauga.

It is nearly time for dress parade, and I must close.

Your affectionate brother, George

IN HIS LAST LETTER before leaving Chattanooga for Parkersburg and Marietta and a furlough, Corporal Hechler wrote his sister on January 14, 1864:

I have read the notices you spoke of in your letter. They are in the main true as far as I know, a little highly colored perhaps. As for the regiment being in the lead where it speaks about it, they might as well say the whole army was. Perhaps this officer was in the lead of their regiment as far as any, but that's no sign they are better than others or the regiment better if they don't get ahead of others. I know of the party which followed General Reynolds chasing the Rebels as far as Chickamauga (about 150 strong), but few were from the 92nd. I don't think there was one for each company.

I received the thread in your letter safely. You need not send any more for the present, as I have re-enlisted and shall probably be home on a furlough soon. Six of Company G only have re-enlisted. I don't know how many of the regiment. We have not been mustered yet. I don't know how long it will be, as they are mustering such first that keep up their organization as regiments. This requires three-fourths of the men present for duty.

The weather is getting a little warmer here and the ground is muddy on top but frozen underneath.

Yesterday afternoon one engine and a few empty cars came into town from below, so it seems that the road is nearly finished. No loaded train has arrived yet.

Uncle Sam is going to bridge the Tennessee River at this place, and the 36th is working at the bridge now. This relieved us from picket duty.

Your affectionate brother, George

EARLY IN 1864, a short and trim Corporal in Union blues named George Hechler came home to Parkersburg and Marietta. This was a special furlough which members of the 36th Ohio Volunteer Infantry Regiment received prior to re-enlistment.

The weather was mild for February when Cpl. Hechler reached Parkersburg. The ice was just breaking up in the Ohio, Little Kanawha and Muskingum Rivers and the current carried the ice blocks down from upstream.

In Parkersburg, the Wood county commissioners—H.P. Dils, L.A. Beckwith, Henderson Deem, John Hannaman and G. S. Henry, were getting ready for the town elections in Walker, Lubeck, Williamstown, Belleville and surrounding communities. Editorially, The Parkersburg Gazette of January 21, 1864, noted that Union sentiment was solidifying in the brand new state of West Virginia: "The effect of close protection for the last six months has changed the feeling and condition of a large portion of our people who were wavering and doubtful. Many who were secessionists a year ago have now put themselves in a true Union position, and guerrillas have been discouraged and are returning to their homes and trying to make their peace with their neighbors. We may now regard West Virginia as nearly as purified as any of the border states, and although taxes cannot yet be collected in all portions for various causes, we feel that we are fast approaching peace."

Picking up a copy of The Gazette, Cpl. Hechler could read the fiery lines of the patriotic poem carrying these stirring words:

> Cast the traitors from thy breast
> Let this motto of the West
> Blazoned on each banner be
> Mountaineers are always free!

The editor of The Gazette had his troubles in those days, which shone through the following, little item which appeared in the January 28, 1864 issue: "We are told that we should have announced the juvenile concert that took place under the charge of Siegfried as from the Methodist, not Southern Methodist Church. We understood him to say the 'Southern' Church, and we do not know that it makes much difference."

After the editor had made his apologies a little less than humble, he counterattacked in an item directly below this, which read as follows: "Persons who want notices published in this paper must write them out and hand them into the office. We do not profess to know everybody's business and we will not publish any more matters that are just given us verbally in the street. This is one of the reforms we will have."

THE PARKERSBURG TO which Corporal Hechler returned in early 1864 was a fast-growing city.

The Oil business was still booming and the docks and railroad did a thriving trade. Midway in his furlough, Hechler could read on February 18, 1864, that "The first National Bank at Parkersburg is now nearly prepared for operation. Another week will complete the work on the vault and room and the bank will then be opened."

The city was looking forward to a prosperous future. The same issue carried an editorial which read in part: "Amid the collisions of man with man, our state was formed and we became a star in the galaxy of states. Amid this same star, Parkersburg has become a city doubled in population and productive industry. It has been the general belief that the time will come when Parkersburg will be the great commercial emporium of West Virginia, and a manufacturing point of importance."

From Parkersburg, Corporal Hechler crossed the Ohio River and went over to Marietta and hence to his little hill farm atop Harmar Hill. The rude log house somehow seemed strangely empty without Brother John, still missing in action and not heard from after the bloody battle of Chickamauga. Embracing his favorite sister Kate silently, it was not long before the young corporal had doffed his blues, took an axe and a cross-cut saw, and ventured out into the late winter slush on the farm to do a little clean-up work. The Army had made him restless, with a compulsion to be doing something constructive all the time, and he wanted to forget the deep loneliness and sorrow he felt about his Brother John.

THE FEBRUARY DAYS of 1864 were idyllic days for Cpl. Hechler, as he spent his furlough prior to re-enlistment at the home and hearth of family and friends in Marietta and Parkersburg. But the inevitable day of return to camp arrived, and there were many tearful goodbyes at the Harmar Depot.

One of the boys from the 28th Ohio Volunteer Infantry Regiment didn't quite make it on the day of return. As Corporal Hechler wrote, "Sam A. did not go to Columbus till Monday. He had his transportation to pay-half-fare. He says he came to the depot at

Harmar Saturday morning in time to see the train go up the grade outside of town."

From Louisville, Kentucky, on March 11, 1864, Corporal Hechler wrote to his sister Kate in Marietta:

> I will try and write you a few lines as we have a nice place here. We are at the Soldiers Home here. We came down from Cincinnati last night on the General Buell. We have a better place here than we have ever been in when together soldiering. I do not know whether we will get away from here today or not.
>
> We have had a very nice time so far. The first day was rather cold and disagreeable coming from Marietta to Columbus.
>
> If you had seen some of the boys who were married while at home since we left Harmar till this morning, you would rather pity than envy their young wives. One of them is sorry he got married: says he was a fool for doing it: would not do it again for the best woman in the world, but says he was so drunk he did not know what he was doing. Are not his wife's prospects bright for a happy future?
>
> Sunday we went to Camp Chase. Left it again Tuesday evening and started for Cincinnati in an extra train about 2 o'clock Wednesday morning. All but the one car we were in was filled with recruits for different regiments. They had preaching at Camp Chase both evenings we were there, by a Chaplain who had come in from the front and was just on his way home.
>
> Wednesday afternoon I went to the Western Museum in Cincinnati. There are some things there worth seeing, but it is not as interesting as the museum at Le Havre, France. Thursday afternoon we started for this place. At Cincinnati, we met Lt. Mitchell and four men. He was Acting Adjutant while Cherrington had been at home. He thought he would find the regiment at Chattanooga when we got there. They have had no promise yet to go to West Virginia, but think they will get to go.
>
> The repulse of the Brigade, or the fault of it, is laid on the gallant (?) 92nd at Chattanooga. It was ordered to support the 11th in their charge, but instead of moving promptly to their support when they became hotly engaged, the 92nd faced about and tried to put safe distance between themselves and the Rebels,

leaving the 11th to be out-numbered, outflanked and finally compelled to fall back with a loss of 30 or 40 killed—so goes the story among officers that ought to know what they say.

I saw one man in Cincinnati who said he was one of the lot escaped from Danville Prison. He only came in a few days ago. Negroes fed him altogether, and piloted him most of the way. He does not think Brother John was among them.

We have just had dinner: at the table I sat by the side of a man who has only lately joined our Army. He started from his home in Dixie one day after the Danville prisoners escaped. He says he belonged to Lee's Army; 14 of his company started at the same time, and all have joined our Army now. He says that the Rebel Army will in a manner disband this Spring when their soldiers' time is out. If they cannot get good terms, they will accept poor ones. He says there was not even corn enough to eat in the South. Perhaps he exaggerated a little, but he seemed truthful and intelligent enough.

Brother George

42. Religion Had Deep Meaning

No Atheists — Nine Did Not Re-enlist

THERE ARE NO ATHEISTS in the trenches in any war, and this was particularly true in the Civil War. For Corporal Hechler, religion had a deep meaning which the field of combat made even more personal. He wrote his sister Kate in Marietta in the spring of 1864:

> This forenoon I was to church over in Ringgold. A brick meeting house is used for services, that was never finished. The walls are up and the roof on. The windows are there, or rather frames, for nearly all the glass is broken and boards nailed up to keep the wind and rain out. There is a good floor laid, but the seats consist of hewn timbers raised onto blocks of wood at each end. The house was nearly full. There was one old lady there, and all the rest were soldiers belonging to the infantry and artillery, from privates to captains. If you could look on such a congregation during prayer you would soon see that more than one denomination was represented, as some kneel, some sit and some stand up. There was prayer meeting, and then preaching. I do not know the denomination of the chaplain who preached but it was a very good sermon.
>
> Should my body fill a soldier's grave or lay unburied; may I not hope to soon see our good Mother then, who has gone before, where sorrow is no more? I hope, dear sister, we will all meet there, where parting will be no more, if not permitted to meet again here on earth, but my hope is disturbed by many doubts regarding myself.

FOR A FEW WEEKS during March and April, 1864, prior to returning to camp in Charleston, W. Va. Cpl. Hechler was stationed near Ringgold, Ga., close to Chattanooga, Tennessee. Writing to Sister Kate on March 17, 1864, he said:

> I will try and write a short letter to you this warm afternoon, although the last few nights have been very cold and disagreeable. I wrote a letter from Louisville on the 11th, the same afternoon we started for Nashville, where we arrived on the 12th and found the regiment in the barracks on their way home. There are nine men of Company G who did not re-enlist that could. We had to come to the front, though, as they said we had had our furlough. Some of the men spoke of going back, but all came along without any trouble.
>
> I went to the theater that night. Over half of our detachment went. The house was so crowded there were not seats enough for all the people. Most of them were soldiers. The evening seemed to pass fast for me, but I did not think it would be worth as much as 25 cents to me.
>
> The day afterward, on the 12th, we started from Nashville for Chattanooga. The distance is 151 miles and it took us 24 hours to travel over the distance on account of some delays. This was not the easiest or most agreeable part of our visit home, as there were 51 of us in one freight car and nobody was allowed to go on top. However, the boys were in good spirits when we arrived in Chattanooga. We expected to find the rest of the regiment in the old camp, but were disappointed. Only a few convalescents were left, and the camp torn down and carried off. The others had started to report at the front. We drew some rations in the evening, and started for Ringgold the next morning about 10 o'clock, and marched over 18 miles before dark. My knapsack felt a little awkward and my feet got some sore before evening. However, I got along very well-better than I had expected I would be. We are now a camp by ourselves.
>
> Yesterday all the men that belonged to the 36th joined us again. We have a battalion here now, as with recruits and all we have about 275 men present. Some are still coming up. Captain

Stanley is in command. He is the only officer along. The companies are in charge of sergeants.

The most part of today is being spent in fixing and cleaning camp. Everything is quiet here as far as I know. Only once or twice I believe the Rebels have disturbed our pickets since the army has been here.

There is not one family living on the road between Chattanooga and this place. Most of the houses are torn down and fences burnt, so that the country looks more like a wilderness than a place that only lately was settled by people pretending to be farmers. I have not been lonesome yet since I have started out this last time, but we have not had much leisure time yet.

A FEW WEEKS LATER, on April 3, 1864, Corporal Hechler wrote to his sister in Marietta:

I will try and write you a few lines this pleasant Sabbath afternoon. We have had but few nice days since we came down here. We had several snow storms. At one time the snow was about eight inches deep and it took several days to melt it off, but we do not worry very much about cold as we are camped right in the woods so that we have plenty of wood handy to build good fires.

There are about 270 men present here who belong to the 36th Regiment. We are under command of Captain Stanley. Company G is under command of Sergeant M. C. True. We have guard duty to do about once a week, but it is easy.

I have not seen a Rebel since I came down here. I do not think there are many deserters coming in now. The railroad is finished some distance beyond Ringgold. This seems as though the Army here would have to advance soon. But there are no troops here of any note scarcely. So I do not see that we could do much if there were Rebels to oppose us, and General Johnston is reported to have 50,000 men in our front. There is some talk of this detachment starting for West Virginia soon, but there is nothing certain about it yet, and we may have to stay down here this summer.

John G. Riggs was moved to Libby Prison not very long ago, but I could not find out anything about Brother John.

The 31st Ohio has not come up yet as they cannot get transportation from Nashville. Their furloughs expired one day after ours. They had started to march through, but had only got to Murfreesboro a few days ago.

I am getting along very well. Feel better contented here than I did at home. I have had very good health ever since I started from there and thinking I am doing my duty to the country of my adoption, I can rest satisfied, come what may.

Give my love to the folks at home and to Cousins Kate, Hannah and Rose Ann, as I suppose you will see all of them sometime.

Your affectionate brother, George

43. Transfer to West Virginia

Nice Times — Quitting George
Sharp Skirmishing — Familiar Ground

BACK TO WEST VIRGINIA! This enthusiastic cry went up from all the men of the 36th Ohio Volunteer Infantry Regiment as they broke camp in northern Georgia, headed for Cincinnati via the Tennessee and Ohio Rivers, and thence went by boat to Point Pleasant and up the Kanawha to Charleston, W. Va. in May, 1864.

In his last letter from camp in Ringgold, Ga., April 13, 1864, Cpl. Hechler wrote to his sister Kate in Marietta:

> I received your letter dated 29th of March a few days ago. The report that Companies C and G are to be consolidated has no truth in it. They have drilled together as one company here what few times we have been out on drill, and perhaps someone wrote that home, which is what started the report. Only the recruits have been drilling this week and I do not think that the others will have to drill much till we join the regiment. There is a rumor here now that we will join the regiment at Camp Dennison to go to the Kanawha Valley from there, to serve as infantry.
>
> We are having very nice times here now, with duty to do only about once a week, and have plenty to eat. Several trains come into this place daily, but there is nothing being stored away here. Several veterans' regiments have come in lately, but there is not much going on now. Last week Major General Thomas ("The Rock of Chickamauga") reviewed our division. Sometimes there is something done after review, so I do not know whether there will be this time or not.

The health of the Army is very good at this time, considering the number of recruits present. One has come up to Company G who enlisted since the boys went home. We have 35 men present in Company G. Two of them are on the sick list, but they are both about.

The last few days here look as though spring meant to come, yet it has been warm even while it rained. The grass begins to look green and the buds on the trees are swelling. As soon as the woods are green, we have the promise of plenty of Rebel deserters, but the few that are coming in now. A few days ago there were several of them in town in the division guardhouse. They appeared to think that the Rebels would give up every other point before they will Richmond. Perhaps they are right.

One member of Company G is now serving out his sentence of court-martial for desertion. It is forfeit all pay and allowances while absent, forfeit twelve months' pay, prepare and make good the time he lost by desertion by serving a period of twelve months after the present term of enlistment has expired, and be confined at hard labor for three months. Double's sentence is not as hard as he was only seven months absent, but that is, I think, all the difference.

AT LAST, EARLY IN MAY, Cpl. Hechler's unit quit Georgia and returned via train and boat to West Virginia. He recalls, in a letter from Charleston, W. Va. on May 14, 1864: "After we left Cincinnati we were very crowded on the boat and the weather was bad. A short distance below Gallipolis a man jumped over board as the boat passed his father's house. Someone came after him with a skiff. A few minutes afterward several more went off with a coal boat, which had been taken along somewhere for coal. At Gallipolis we landed and many more went to see their folks. There are several regiments of militia there. Most of those who went off the boat have just come up."

CONTINUING, CPL. HECHLER in his first letter in many months from West Virginia, wrote his sister in Marietta:

When I wrote my last letter I hardly expected that I would be here at this time, but we are now part of the regiment. All of them that came up the Valley from home are out somewhere with General Crook. No one seems to know where as there is no communication open with Crook. They left this place two weeks ago yesterday.

Two weeks ago we left Ringgold. The day before I was awakened in the morning by the sound of musket-firing and sharp skirmishing was kept up till about 8 o'clock. We expected to have to go into a fight there, when about 7 o'clock a mounted orderly went to Captain Stanley's quarters. We did not like the idea of going into a fight there, as we had got word from Colonel Duval a few days before that the regiment was at Charleston, but it turned out to be the order for us to report at Charleston. Saturday morning we started for Chattanooga afoot. We arrived there early in the afternoon and went to the barracks. Sunday evening we went on the railroad cars and the next morning had reached as far as Stevenson, Alabama. There we took the road past Guntersville to Nashville. Huntsville and Athens are the nicest towns I have yet seen. The country about is nearly level and very rich. Most of the houses are large and well-built, many of them very costly and a good number of them have several acres of ground around them, planted with shade trees, shrubbery and flowers.

There is considerable cotton planted in northern Alabama, along the line of the railroad. There is not much corn planted there. Most of the hands working are Negro women and children, scarcely large enough to look over the plough-handles. A few men are left yet, but I did not see one able-bodied Negro working in the fields. At Nashville we had to take a boat. There were several families of refugees from East Tennessee on the same boat coming North as Sherman had forbidden any more rations to be issued to civilians, and there is not much left to live on. They are forced to move north or starve.

While we were coming along the railroad in Alabama, the Army was moving South and trains of refugees north. Many of their wagons had two and three yoke of cattle hitched to them, but they looked very bony.

While we were in Cincinnati the draft was coming off there, and the news from the East was very encouraging.

For the balance of 1864, Cpl. Hechler was in West Virginia, moving from Charleston to the eastern panhandle, and occasionally crossing the border for the sharp fighting in northern Virginia. His regiment swung through Parkersburg in the summer months of 1864 on the way east to Martinsburg. By now the first glimmers of the end of the war were appearing on the horizon.

THE 36TH OHIO VOLUNTEER Infantry Regiment was back on old familiar stamping ground in the spring of 1864. "We are camped on the opposite side of the Kanawha River from Charleston," wrote Cpl. Hechler on May 15, 1864. "The river is rising very fast today, so that it is almost impossible to cross from one side to the other: and it is still raining. Last night about one regiment of militia came up the river and went up further today. There is some talk today of detailing provost guards from our detachment for Charleston. If that is true, it would seem as though we would stay here for some time."

But fate did not keep Col. Hechler near Charleston and the Kanawha river for very long. As the spring and summer of 1864 wore on, the regiment became engaged in some of their bitterest fighting of the entire Civil War in raids and sharp engagements in the Shenandoah Valley.

The 36th Regiment, recruited largely from the Marietta area, had its ups and downs as several regimental commanders were shot out of action by the Confederates. Finally, in the spring of 1864 the first regimental commander and beloved tight-lipped Indian fighter General Cook returned to the Kanawha Valley to take command of the 36th and other fighting units of the Union Army in the area.

"The people back home have been petitioning President Lincoln to send me back to West Virginia." General Crook wrote, "Grant told me he had passed a wish of the President to have me go back to that country, but another demand had just been sent, and I was informed I would have to go this time. Just then General Grant had been made Lieutenant General, and said he would like to have me East."

For the troops of the 36th, it was a wonderful break to have

General Crook back in their midst, for although he was a strict disciplinarian, they had implicit faith in his leadership. Even if he was now too important a general to command a regiment, the mere fact that General Crook was close by gave a tremendous lift to the men of the 36th.

Meanwhile, Corporal Hechler in his May 15 letter from Charleston, W. Va., was deeply concerned about the fate of his Brother John, yet tried to cheer up his sister and allay her fears for John's safety. "I wrote a letter to you yesterday up in the office." Cpl. Hechler wrote his sister in Marietta:

> . . . but as Duston gave me one from you in the evening that contained one from Brother John besides. I will try and answer it today, although I have nothing particular to do.
>
> I am glad to hear that John (from his letter) is well yet, and I hope to see him soon, free from captivity once more. As for sending a box to him. I do hardly think that it can be done now, but if you should send anything send woolen clothes as near our Army uniform as you can get, as citizen's clothes are in most cases confiscated. Use as much of my money as you need.
>
> I saw by the paper a few days ago that two of the boys of our company are in the hospital at Annapolis. They are James Oliver and George Linton.
>
> I am thankful that John's health has been preserved so far. The firm belief of the men in Company G is that John will come back all right. I have not heard one man say anything about him if he was told that John was a prisoner, but would lightly say, 'Oh, he will stand it,' or 'he will come out all right.' This feeling of security in others, I believe, helped me along considerably.
>
> I think you are right in your ideas of discharging our duties to Our Heavenly Father.
>
> Tell Willie Fisher that Cousin George will be there as soon as he can, and give him more music if he will be a good boy till he comes.
>
> Give my love to all inquiring friends—and much love to yourself from,
>
> Your affectionate brother, George

44. Jenkins Killed at Cloyd's Mountain

Confederates Routed — Natural Bridge

IN THE SPRING and early summer of 1864, the 36th Ohio Volunteer Infantry Regiment started from their old camping ground near Charleston, West Virginia, on a raid to Dublin Depot on the Virginia and Tennessee Railroad. The old and first commander of the regiment, General George Crook, was now the brigade commander of many additional forces, including the Ohio Valley boys in the 36th.

General Crook moved his fighting men out of camp via the Falls of Kanawha, Raleigh, and Princeton. At Princeton, they had a sharp skirmish with the Confederates, but a bigger and more significant battle took place at Cloyd's Mountain. There the Union troops drove the Confederates from their positions and captured or destroyed a large amount of Rebel property, including locomotives, siege guns, work-shops, and destroyed the railroad bridge across the New River.

Even more significant was the fact that the battle of Cloyd's Mountain resulted in the mortal wounding of Confederate General Albert Gallatin Jenkins. Jenkins was one of the most brilliant young soldiers-statesmen of the Ohio Valley. A graduate of Marshall (now Marshall University), an outstanding lawyer, he had represented what is now West Virginia's Fourth Congressional District (plus some additional counties) in the House of Representatives for two terms. He was in his early thirties when he fell at the battle of Cloyd's Mountain. It was a tragic loss for the Confederates and for the statesmanship of the Ohio Valley.

Writing from Charleston, W. Va., after his return from the rigorous expedition, Corporal Hechler noted to his sister:

> Tomorrow is the fourth day of July. The news from the battle fields is not cheering as it was one year ago, but our prospects for a dinner are much better than they were in Tennessee then, as some of us had only black beans to eat that day, others nothing but green apples.
>
> I have been looking for a letter from you ever since we came in from our last raid, but have not seen any yet, so I thought I would write one this afternoon. I commenced writing day before yesterday, but my hand sweated so badly that I had to give it up because the paper got wet.
>
> Our Company is camped in town near General Crook's headquarters. It has been detached from the Regiment and mounted to act as the General's escort. He is now commanding this Department. Major General Hunter and staff left town this forenoon with the good wishes of most of the troops here for a long and safe journey to some other place, and a good, long stay.
>
> We are having very hot and dry weather here now, but not much duty to do besides taking care of our horses which, by the way, is something new to us, and as they are poor horses, takes a good part of our time. We got horses first at Lexington, part of our company-I got one there. The next day we marched on the road passing about five miles from the Natural Bridge. All of General Crook's staff was around to see it (the General did not go); our Company went along. It is a sight worth seeing.
>
> This last has been the hardest trip I have been on yet, and I think did a considerable amount of damage to the Rebels on railroads alone. Besides that we lived off the country nearly altogether, and you may imagine how much was left along the roads. After we commenced retreating from before Lynchburg, however, some of the troops fared very poorly as the country through which we came was poor and our rear followed closely by the Rebels for three or four days. The first day at noon Captain Blaser's Company of scouts and Company G had a race of about a mile with the Rebel Cavalry, for a gap in the mountain.

The column had stopped for dinner and we were ordered back to hold the Rebels in check. As the Infantry moved out, they planted a battery and fired-a few shots-so as to get the range on the road.

At the same time, a party of their Cavalry worked themselves around our left flank. After the troops had all started, we left the hill we had been stationed on, but had to ride through the woods so as to keep out of their cannons' mouth. The Rebs came to the pass about the same time with us, but their firing had no effect, so that nobody was lost on our side. Some of our boys dismounted and took to the woods for a little while. Rebel prisoners said afterwards that they lost two killed there. You will see all the particulars of this raid in the papers, so I will not write anything more about it.

George Linton, who was a prisoner for some time with Brother John, has been exchanged and is now here with the Company, James Oliver died at Annapolis, Maryland, from the effects of prison life.

I am well and hope these few lines will find you well and enjoying yourself.

Your affectionate brother, GEORGE

45. The Front Lines at Shenandoah

Union Army Strong — John's Death Certain
Generals Crook and Kelly Captured at Headquarters
Conf. General Jubal Early and 1,800 Men Captured

IN THE SUMMER OF 1864, the Confederates still had plenty of fight left in them, particularly, when their homeland was invaded, Rebel General Early, and one of Parkersburg's great contributions to the Civil War Confederate General "Mudwall" Jackson, stormed up from Richmond into the Shenandoah Valley and drove the Union forces back into West Virginia.

After a long and harrowing retreat over the mountains into camp at Charleston, Corporal Hechler and his buddies of the 36th Ohio Volunteer Infantry received the welcome news that once again they would return to Parkersburg. On July 12, 1864, the entire regiment boarded steamers at Charleston for the pleasant trip down the Kanawha and up the Ohio River. The artillery moved overland to Parkersburg while the infantry enjoyed a restful boat trip.

It was hay making time as the Union boys in blue moved through Putnam, Mason, Jackson and up through Wood county. Women and children everywhere were raking or loading the hay under the direction of a few very old men, since nearly all the able bodied men were serving in the Army.

The hope for seeing much of Parkersburg and Marietta were dashed quickly as the troops boarded the train to Martinsburg and back to the Shenandoah Valley front lines. From Harpers Ferry on July 30, 1864, after some brisk fighting, Corporal Hechler finally had a chance to write Sister Kate in Marietta about his bitter experience in the Shenandoah.

THIS WAS THE FIRST time that this battle-hardened regiment had turned its back on the enemy, and it was a painful event for Corporal Hechler to chronicle:

> I want you to excuse me for not writing sooner, although we had not much chance since we left Parkersburg, as we have been travelling or fighting most of the time. Our company has not done much fighting, and during the retreat from Winchester to Martinsburg we were with the rear. Company G lost one man wounded.
>
> You have perhaps heard about all the fights the troops under General Crook have been engaged in. Part of the infantry was engaged at Snickers Ferry, and some of them behaved very badly, especially a detachment of dismounted cavalry. The 175th Ohio was in that fight and some of them did well, for raw troops. The first and second brigade of Crook's old Division had not gotten up yet. They marched by way of Charleston, up the Shenandoah Valley toward Winchester.
>
> The First Brigade had a fight near Charleston; the 36th lost a few men there. General Averill's cavalry and the 2nd brigade pushed on to Winchester, where the Rebels made a stand and were badly whipped, losing four pieces of artillery. Captain Blaser's and Cherrington's companies were within miles of Winchester on the same evening of the fight, but the Rebels were picketing the road we were on and we did not try to drive them away as we did not wish to fight just then without knowing how Averill was getting along.
>
> At night we came back to Snickers Ferry, and started for Harpers Ferry shortly after daylight, with General Crook and Lt. Patton. We did not know for what purpose till we saw Crook in the evening wear two stars. At night we went back to where we had left the troops in the morning about 23 miles from Harpers Ferry. Friday we marched to Winchester, Saturday we had skirmishing all day; and Sunday the Rebels attacked us about 10

Lt. Jonathan N. Patton

o'clock a.m. Soon after, our company was ordered out and deployed to keep stragglers back with the command-or rather keep them up to the front. But our line was falling back, the Rebels coming on, getting so that it soon became impossible to do anything with them. Officers commanding companies came away with most of their men so that it looked more like flight that retreat, till after we had come back three or four miles where the Rebel cavalry charged the road ahead of the troops falling back in line. This started all the stragglers out of sight on the double-quick at short notice.

Generals Averill and Dunfee followed them with all the mounted men they could gather, so they had no time to do any mischief besides scaring stragglers and teamsters. This is the only cavalry charge I ever saw made, and it was almost harmless-at least what I could see of it. Part of the time I couldn't see much, not even my horse's head, on account of dust, but you will see all the particulars in the papers.

I am well and hope these few lines will find; you stout and enjoying good health again. Be cheerful, for there are good times coming, but should we never meet on earth again, let us try to meet where parting will be no more. Give my love to the folks at home and all enquiring friends—and keep a good share for yourself, from

Your affectionate brother, GEORGE

On October 22, 1864, George wrote Kate about liquor and cool weather:

Martinsburg, West Virginia
October 22, 1864

Dear Sister:

There was twelve of us came down here last night, escort for Captain Craig. He came down here on some business, and brought the horses and other property of Captain Bier's, General Crook's Adjutant General who was killed a few days ago in the fight at Cedar Creek, to this place to be sent home I suppose.

This last fight has been the hardest fought in the Valley this summer and the Rebels now most demoralized. In the evening Crook's command was surprised in camp, or nearly so, the blame of it all, according to reports, rests on Colonel Thornburn, commanding First Division. He was mortally wounded in the fight.

I must tell you an incident, rather laughable now, but might have been serious, that happened last night. Some sentries were at Bunker Hill as we came along last night about two o'clock, and ordered Captain Craig and his escort under arrest. He then ordered us to give up our arms. We suspected foul play and only turned the muzzles of our guns toward him. Somebody then got a light and he showed some papers he had, and one officer was with us that knew him. By this time some of our troops came along and he concluded to let us go on. Somebody said the cause of all that talking was spirits. This valley seems to be a bad place for such articles. The Rebels say Early was drunk when he lost the fight.

The weather is getting quite cool. Have you heard anything lately from brother John? How is Cousin Jack getting along? Has he been drafted yet, or is Rose not going to give him up?

George

On November 19, 1864, George wrote to his sister from Martinsburg, West Virginia:

There is news here at present that the Army is camped near Winchester, but the Rebels seem to be afraid since their defeat of last month at Cedar Creek to risk another battle. We are in hopes of spending the winter at Cumberland, if we get into winter quarters at all.

I am well satisfied with the results of the election, for it will prevent foreign intervention and show to the Rebels the determination of the people of the north to preserve their government at any cost.

The war may not close for some time yet, for the leaders of the rebellion will hold out as long as they can persuade or force a man to fight for them, but Jeff Davis says: "Two-thirds of our Army are absent, the most of them without leave." Nearly half of them are in our ranks, and our Army is as strong today, if not stronger, than it ever was. Have the Rebels then any reasonable prospect of success? Sherman is about to show the people of Georgia—if reports are true—that A. H. Stephens, their present Vice President, knew what he spoke about at Macon in 1861, and may we not hope they will heed his advice in 1864? (He vigorously opposed secession.)

ON NOVEMBER 30, 1864, George wrote to his sister from Camp Russell near Greentown, West Virginia:

I have not seen the returns from this Army, only in part, and cannot say much about how it voted. Companies G and E of the 36th voted at the 91st O.V.I. as the rest of the Regiment was on its way to Martinsburg as train guard on election day. The cars run in five miles of Winchester now and today we have yesterday's papers in camp. This is getting news in reasonable time.

Sam Atkinson was here yesterday to our quarters. He is well. Says he has not had any letters from home for some time. Was going to write today.

There is a report that the 36th is going to the Kanawha soon. We have been looking to get to Cumberland, but there is no sign of any move about Headquarters. The Baltimore and Ohio Railroad is reported out by the Rebels and most of our Cavalry has gone out.

From Camp Russell on December 19, 1864, George wrote to Kate:

All of the Army of West Virginia except Headquarters broke camp this morning and marched toward the rear. I do not think though that they are going very far, for the wagons were loaded with lumber of their quarters.

The weather is very bad this morning. It has been raining ever since before daylight, and as there was a big snow melted off in the last few days, there is plenty of mud here and some to spare.

Captain Cherrington is here yet, well and attending to his duties. Among them are taking care of Rebel deserters. A few of them are coming in every day.

I do not know what is the reason Major Palmer has resigned unless he is tired of the service, but the most of the officers of the 36th have resigned or are about to do so, and there are not men enough to have vacancies filled, nor is the recruiting . . . General Crook says it shall not be consolidated, so what he intends to do with it I don't know.

The only way we could reasonably expect to hear anything from brother John would be to write to Annapolis, Maryland. I have been thinking about writing for several days past, but did not know how to direct. I shall find out and write to Annapolis the first opportunity, and you can write to Columbus if you wish to. I have not given up yet to hope of hearing from him.

Do not try to conceal in your letters what kind of spirits you are in, because you cannot, and it will only be so much harder on your body. Cheer up dear sister or do you think that more misfortune has fallen to your lot than you will be able to bear? Labor no such thoughts. God in His wisdom doeth all things well. He knows your strength and will help to bear out our burdens if we ask Him. I know it but ill becomes me to speak so to you, who I feel sure, is better and asks oftener than I do, but I feel like saying it.

Martin Schnary is well. I told him what you said in your letter. Have your fortune told if you can. I had mine told at Charleston in July, but there was not much truth in what the fortune teller said, only about the immediate future that has now passed some time. I was in the country at the time and had it done for curiosity. I have no faith in them.

From Cumberland, Maryland, George wrote to Kate on January 4, 1865:

> Happy New Year to you Kate:
>
> This is a pretty time for it, you will say, but this is the first time I have had an opportunity of wishing you a happy New Year, and someone has said "better late than never" and so I thought in this case.
>
> We have come, I think, to a place at last where winter quarters will be put up for us. About twenty carpenters commenced work on them today. We marched to this place from Winchester, a little over 100 miles, in four days, but spent nearly one of them crossing the Potomac at Williamsport, as there was nothing but a small ferry boat to cross in, and the river too high to ford. We came on the National Road West. It runs alternately through Maryland and Pennsylvania, in the mountains.
>
> About ten miles from Cumberland I saw a deer, not running away, but taking a sleigh ride to market, I suppose, for it was dead. We arrived here about two o'clock Saturday afternoon, and we were glad of it, for you may imagine we had no pleasure trip across the snow and ice covered mountains. At present we are quartered in a church, doing Provost duty, which, by the way, is not the most agreeable. I was on duty last night, and got but one hour's rest till five in the morning. There were two balls in town, at one of them a row was got up, and four men shot. I saw but one of them and helped carry him to the hospital after we cleared the house. From the other place word came that trouble was brewing. We then went and broke it up at once. So much for the commencement.
>
> Have you ever received the 40 dollars I sent by Captain Kelly? Or the letter containing the five dollar bill you had sent me, as we had been paid off before I got it I did not need it and started back a few days afterward.
>
> I have written to Annapolis to find out something about brother John, if possible, but have not received any answer yet.
>
> I will send a picture in this of the Chaplain of the 5th Va. He gave us one apiece the night before we left Camp Russell.

From Cumberland, George writes Kate on January 10, 1865:

We are still quartered in the Presbyterian Church. Our barracks will be finished tomorrow or next day. I shall be glad of it, for we can then get out of this dirt, noise and confusion, as there will be ten rooms for us instead of the little over half a one we have here. Of course, not as large as this one.

We are on duty now nearly every other day, but I think we will not have as much to do after the troops that are camped near the city will have their quarters built. At present the most of our two companies are having them. We pay fifty cents a week and then have vegetables furnished us besides our regular rations. There are ten of us boarding at one house, and I believe rather than cook themselves would pay double the amount they are paying now.

FROM CUMBERLAND on January 13, 1865, George wrote to Kate:

I received your letter dated 4th inst., one number of the Atlantic Monthly and Daily Times, each yesterday. This news of brother John's death came unexpected to me. I have not heard anything from Annapolis yet. Will you tell me in your next letter how you got the news, and all you know about the circumstances and time of his death? It may be hard for you to write about it, but I shall not believe the report till convinced of the fact by a report from one that occupies a position to know all about the case.

On January 23, 1865, George wrote to Kate:

I have received the letter in which you said how you had heard about John's death. There is scarcely a chance for any doubt left, for G. J. Hinton ought to know what he says, and whatever he says I should not one moment doubt. It is hard to lose a dear Brother thus, but perhaps it is all for the best, the Lord only knoweth, and He doeth all things well. I do not feel in the least revengeful toward the Rebels, not a particle more than

I have before, but my determination to fight till the end of the struggle (if permitted to live that long) is as strong as ever. I know that the right must in the end triumph, and are we not engaged in a fight for the right and justice against oppression and every kind of wrong? I would not have you understand this as alluding merely to slavery, but many other acts perpetrated by the now leading Rebels. Although I am glad to see slavery go down with the power of the rebellion, I believe the day is not far distant when peace will again return to this land and find it better and more worthy than when the bloody monster War drove it from our borders.

I had a trip to Albany, New York, last week. Captain Mitchell, myself and four men went to take one Robinson who had been a surgeon in the Army, but had been caught and sentenced to one year hard labor in the penitentiary for swindling the Government. We started about midnight Tuesday night and came back Saturday morning. We passed through both Philadelphia and New York after night. I was anxious to be there in daytime to see if I could remember the looks of any place, but was disappointed. At Albany we crossed the Hudson River on the ice in a sleigh. I do not know how thick the ice was, but there was a sort of plank road or bridge built down on each side for the teams to get down over the bank on.

Here is what George wrote to Kate on January 28, 1865:

I received your letter dated the 18th inst. a few days ago. He came here today on his way to Annapolis. There is no room left to doubt the truth of the reported death of brother John. It seems hard but no doubt is for the best. Let us trust that he is where there is no strife, no sorrowing nor sighing, where our darling Mother has been called long ago. Long? It seems but yesterday we stood around her dying bed, received her farewell kiss and blessing. Do you remember when John said he would not kiss the baby only on Mother's arms? He was but three years old then. Lived to be twenty-one, and is now dead some time. How time flies! Let us, dear Sister, try and live so that we may all meet in Heaven, if not permitted to again on earth.

I do hardly blame Father for wanting the money. He will hardly forget John while it lasts. There will be about 450 dollars coming.

I do not think you egotistical nor selfish for speaking of yourself. I know that it is hard to bear grief alone, without some kind of sympathizing friend, and who is better to be a friend except your brother? Besides Him that dwelleth on high?

I like Cumberland very well as a place to stay while soldiering. We have all that we could ask for here. But give me the country. I care not if wild woods to live in. I do not know why it is, but I care little for society, though one would think after being in the Army so long a person would like it.

The weather is very cold here, but we are very well protected from it in our houses. There is but three of us staying in the room that I stay in at present. One is at home on furlough, J. C. Parker. By the by, I had forgotten I believe to tell you that I wishes him to bring my watch. His time is up and I hope you let him have the watch if he calls for it.

Two have their wives here in town and stay with them. We have good stove and plenty of coal to build fires with. There have been a great many troops passing through here lately from Thomas' Army going East. It is reported in town today that five Rebel Commissioners have arrived in Washington City yesterday with power to treat for peace on any terms. This last I can hardly believe. I do not think that H. Davis and his comrades in rebellion are that badly frightened while they see Lee before Richmond holding Grant at bay. But the time will sooner or later come now I think that they will hold out for terms as long as there is the least chance for then to do so.

(An article attached to the letter: "A peace conference was held in Hampton Roads in February, 1865, but achieved nothing because Davis still insisted on recognition of right of secession.")

On January 31, 1865, George wrote to Kate:

Captain Cherrington brought my watch through all right, and told me you are well.

G. J. Hinton stopped here from Saturday till this morning, and he told me the particulars about brother John. There can be no more doubt about his death.

His case was one reason to make me doubt the report, as the first letter of yours that I received about it did not say how you had heard it, and he, Hinton, had been reported dead in the papers, but we had heard of his return at the Company.

The picture that I sent represents a truthful scene. The Chaplain of the 5th Va. is a good singer. He carries an instrument to make music with him and sometimes he gives out meetings to sing for the boys as he says, when he generally sings hymns and patriotic songs, and talks a little as he expresses himself, he has some hymns and songs written off in large print letters, he will hand them up in view of the men and invite all to help him sing, just a little. This meeting generally draws large crowds together.

You wish to know how I bear this blow. I can hardly tell you, but assure you it is hard enough. I am trying to do my duty to my country, I fear, better than God, though not very hard, but I have continually to reproach myself with neglect of duty to God. Sometimes even have to accuse myself of cowardice in the cause of the Savior. Why is it?

On February 6, 1865, George wrote to Kate:

J. C. Parker is Sergeant in Company G. He lives in Ludlow Township, Washington County, when he is at home. The man that brought you the last letter is Sergeant J. R. Young, of Company G. I should have said something about him in the letter, but I had intended to send it by mail but while I was doing it up he came into the room and said he had got furlough. Parker then said, "now George you can send your letter right through by John," and Young said he would carry it if I wanted him to. I told him to carry it.

The weather here has been very cold and disagreeable till within a few days past. The wind has blown very hard but not very cold. Day before yesterday it actually blew a hole through a seven inch board in our rooms,. At this would seem like an incredible story, perhaps I had better tell you how it was done, for fear you will think I am yarning. The Lieutenant's quarters stand just above ours. A gust of wind tore one of the boards of his roof off, knocked down his stove pipe and carried the board against our house, the end striking it, knocking a piece out of a board, and driving part of it to the other side of our room, the end of the board then whirled around and knocked one man down who happened to be passing the time. He was the first thing I saw after opening the door, lying among the pieces of barrels. I helped him up; he was stunned and bruised some, but not hurt as the board had struck him broad-side.

There has been a fire in town this evening, but only one small building belonging to the railroad company and used as a storehouse for tools was burned.

I have seen this morning's paper (Baltimore). It reports that the President and Secretary Seward have returned to Washington, and asserts positively that no good has come from their interview with the Rebel Commissioners. This afternoon a rumor was circulated that General Lee has resigned in the Rebel Army, and another that he had surrendered his Army. Good news wouldn't it be? If true.

I hope, however, that peace will soon come. Indeed, I believe it is not very far distant, even if we have to go through another campaign.

ON FEBRUARY 22, 1865, George wrote to Kate, his letter included the news that Generals Crook and Kelly had been captured at their headquarters.

About the one enclosed, I have to say that I know the man. He belongs to the 34th Ohio and has been attached to the Escort as bugler. He calls himself one year older than I am, is a clean soldier, he is good natured when sober, but was drunk several times last fall. He is then very high tempered, almost vicious to persons he does not like. Got mad at me once but would not say anything to me. He had forgotten all about it the next morning. He said some time ago he should never get drunk again, and has, so far, kept his word. We go to church together sometimes, but not every evening. He was raised a Roman Catholic but refuses to go to their church here. He visits the M. E. Church and German Lutheran, but seems to have a decided preference for the latter. His reason for not going to the Catholic church, as he says, is their disloyalty. He is intelligent enough, and if you would write him a letter or two, no doubt you could get to see him, as he expected to go home on furlough soon, near Cincinnati. He has not seen your picture yet, and when Parker told him about you, by the way he praised you up very much, I was present. Told him I should not say anything about him unless asked by you, when I should tell you what you wished to know. He is reading his Testament now. I have not told him about the letter, nor shall I; it is burned up.

I shall try and write a letter home soon. I cannot tell whether I will get a furlough now or not. You have no doubt heard of the capture of Generals Crook and Kelly at their headquarters here in Cumberland. No furloughs are given now or I should have had one about the ides of March. This seems rather a disgraceful affair, but most of the Rebels were here in town, some of them had taken the oath of allegiance the day before and knew all about the place. The sentinels here had been instructed to let everyone pass so that they could come right up to them (as the most of them were dressed in blue), and quietly disarm them, and they actually got both Generals and had left town before the alarm was raised. We saddled our horses soon as we could, but the Rebels had about two hours the start of us. When we left town it was daybreak. At nine o'clock we passed through Romney, Va., 28 miles from this place, where we were only 20 minutes behind them. There was about 70 of them and 50 of us, but our horses began to give out now, one after another dropped out till there was scarcely a dozen left when we got about four miles beyond Romney and in the sights of the Rebs. Two of them had stopped at a house. We got them, but after stopping a few minutes, all of our officers except one drunken Captain, decided to turn back, as we were only poorly armed, had only one or two rounds of ammunition apiece, and the Rebels was more than five to one, if we could overtake them. This Captain called for four volunteers to go with him and charge them. Some told him they would go with a sober but not a drunk man. He has since called the escort cowards. If he stops here in town I fear he will be sorry for it. At Romney coming back, we found the most of the boys. We stopped there about one hour and a half (I got a place there) to rest our horses, we then came on a few miles farther where we found some corn in a field and fed then a little, shortly after sundown we reached Cumberland again, after having ridden about 65 miles the biggest days ride I have ever had on horseback. I feel tired and sore today, as we had not been used to riding.

Today noon 100 guns were fired here, in honor of General Sherman's doings in South Carolina.

In March 6, 1865, letter to Kate, George wrote that General Sheridan had captured General Jubal Early and 1,800 men:

I feel cold and lonesome sometimes, at others I could not be happier, but we must expect to feel pain as well as joy in this world. May we only be found faithful in our trust to Him that has called us and be found faithful servants when we are called to account at the end of our appointed time.

I am well and hope these few lines will find you the same. We are having a report from General Sheridan this morning, that he has captured Early and 1,800 men somewhere up the valley. The report is here that he, Sheridan, started with 25,000 mounted men last week. I hope before long to hear that all the Armies of the rebellion are broke up, so that armed resistance to the Government will soon cease, except by small bands as guerillas, but that kind of warfare could not be carried on long before all country inhabited by then would be a barren waste.

South Carolina is now paying dearly for her secession; her capital in ashes, and doubtless the Army, as it subsists on the country, leaves nothing but wreck and ruin behind it.

The 34th has been transferred to the 36th—that is they came into the 36th much as recruits would, one company to each of the ten, so that the men that formerly belonged to Company G of the 34th still belong to Company G, but now the 36th. Most of the officers have been mustered out of service. Our Company got a Second Lieutenant; the vacancies of non-commissioned officers was filled by such from the 34th; the others have been reduced, but application made to have them mustered out of service. There are about 1,300 men in the 36th now, but only about 700 present for duty, all included.

General Jubal A. Early

On March 8, 1865, George wrote to Kate:

The report about Captain Cherrington drinking is in part correct, but perhaps exaggerated. I do not think there is an officer on the staff now that is a strictly temperate man, indeed but a small minority of officers in the Army. The drunken Captain that I had reference to is Captain Hart of the Ringgold Battalion P. V. Troops. He had been attached to General Kelly's staff. I understand there has been charges preferred against him.

There may be a Court of Inquiry about Crook, but no court martial.

I do hardly think that Father will have to sell his place yet. If I owned it I should not part with it yet, for it is the most valuable mineral land on the run, and if anything is found cannot fail to command a high price I have no idea where he would move to if he sold out.

If you draw that interest in specie and can double it for greenbacks, do so. If not, send it to me if you can safely. I wish you would spite me as you threatened, it would be so funny, and pleasant besides, but I fear you will soon forget your threat and forgive me before you have half revenge.

I must say that I had not tried hard to get furlough. In fact, I did not want one till the middle of this month, but there are no more given now till further orders. You remember what a dull time I was forced to have of it last winter on account of the cold, and I was determined not to go home this winter till there would be prospects of warmer weather.

We had some rain last night and the air today is very warm and sultry for March.

There has been 12 more mounted orderlies and two non-commissioned officers detailed. I am one of them. We are on duty every other day, but have not had much to do yet. I am well yet. There is no sign of our being sent to the Regiment at present. I understand that General Carroll has ordered other arms for us, some fit for an escort, not clubs.

George had the following to report to Kate on March 20, 1865:

General Crook came into town last night. He is not exchanged yet, but only paroled. I have not seen him yet.

It is a disgrace I think to the nation to have a drunkard in the second office of the nation, but intemperance seems to be almost a national sin, even spreading instead of abating. Vice President Johnson no doubt has fallen victim to alcohol, and I fear will not be able to discharge the duties of his office with justice and impartiality as nearly, if not quite all, men's actions given to the use of ardent spirits are governed by their passions instead of judgment.

Captain Cherrington has taken command of the Escort and today the boys are fixing up as though we were going to stay here some time. There is a rumor in the Regiment that they are going West somewhere. I do not know what the Captain came up to the Company for unless he wants to bring them under stricter discipline, as he is still Provost Marshal on the staff.

The sailors do not willingly ship on the Monitors, but they are enlisted for the Naval Service and have no choice of craft, so they will have to go wherever assigned.

I have often thought about the promises of God, that He never requires to bear a heavier burden than He will give us strength to bear, but my faith seems to be very weak indeed.

You must not, dear Sister, think that I am the only friend left to you. Have you not a better and truer friend left?—than any mortal can be? You must not set your heart too much on ever seeing me back, for our life at best is very uncertain and all of us must sooner or later die. When, we do not know, and would it not be much harder for you to get rid of such a belief than it would preventing it to take deep hold of you.

I do sincerely hope that I may be permitted to return home and that soon. There is a good prospect now of the war coming to a close this summer. However, it is still going on and may be prolonged considerable time to come.

On April 1, 1865, George wrote to Kate:

Night before last we had quite a stir in town, but it did not amount to much. The passenger train was captured a short distance East of here and the troops were all ordered out, the rain was pouring down at the time. We did not get outside of town, the Provost guards had been ordered out, and we were to take their places in town, but by some misunderstanding the order came to us to come mounted to Heath's Headquarters, and riding through town stirred the people up considerable.

General Crook looked nearly as well when he came back as he did before he was taken. We can hardly say that we received him, as most of the Escort did not see him till the day he started away again to his new command in the Army of the Potomac. He was going to pay us a visit the day he went away. He had been to see all the rest of the troops.

There is a rumor that Company I is going to the Regiment tomorrow or next day, and G was to be fitted out as Cavalry and sent to Winchester as soon as possible, probably to General Hancock's Headquarters.

46. The Fall of Richmond and the War Nears an End

Lee Surrenders to Grant — President Lincoln Assassinated George Hechler Waits for His Discharge

WHEN THE EXCITING NEWS of the fall of Richmond occurred, here is what George wrote to Kate on April 3, 1865:

> As I am on guard tonight, and everybody seems to be enthusiastic over the news, I thought I might as well write a few lines to you.
>
> Richmond has at last fallen into our possession and before long the Armies of the Rebellion will belong to the things of the past. There was a salute of 100 guns fired here this evening in honor of the victory. Yesterday morning Company I went back to the Regiment. It is to be ready to march Wednesday. There is a rumor tonight that Company G will have to report back for duty, and it is apparently reliable. If that is so, we will have to turn our horses over in the morning and go with the Regiment when it goes.
>
> I have received all the Repositories you sent and read them too. I think that I have spent some hours profitably reading.
>
> Martin Schnary and myself have boxed up some clothes and shall send the box by express to his father, George Schnary. Each article is marked by a piece of paper with the owner's name on it, so that they can easily be told. I may send the receipt in this letter yet, as we intend to send the box in the morning. If Father gets

the clothes of mine and you will be likely to see some of the folks soon—tell them that I want them to keep the overcoat, but do not want any of the other articles.

One man of Company G that deserted last fall has availed himself of the President's Proclamation, and returned for duty today. He left about the first of September last, walked all the way to Canada from the Shenandoah Valley, and has now returned for duty, perhaps a wiser man.

As there was nothing more to do here, but I will not vouch for the truth of the report.

In his first letter since leaving Cumberland for the camp near Princeton, Va., George wrote to Kate on April 12, 1865:

Captain Cherrington handed in his resignation, but General Carroll persuaded him to accept a position on his staff, where he is now. The Company is with the Regiment but the highest point of perfection will be low indeed it would ever acquire under Captain Cherrington or any other man for the boys begin to think that their work as soldiers is almost done and do not want to be made a show of.

I think that early summer will find a large part of our America at home. At least I hope so, but many share in this belief. Now that the Rebels have not only given up Virginia but surrendered their most powerful and best Army, together with its great (?) leader General Lee, to the Army of Grant.

Last night Winchester was partly illuminated. There are still some Rebels in town that look very dark and sullen. Their houses, were of course, closed. Our Chaplain got the use of the Methodist Episcopal Church, had it illuminated, and held a meeting in it. General Carroll and his staff was present. Among those that have lately been exchanged I saw Captain Blaser, the meeting might be called a soldiers mass meeting, as but a few citizens were present.

We have had rain nearly every day since we left Cumberland, and it is really disagreeable today, in shelter tents and dirt now, after having such good quarters all winter, but it is soldiering again.

There is a rumor here that General Carroll said a few days ago that before long his Command would go to Frederick, Md., as there was nothing more to do here, but I will not vouch for the truth of the report.

On April 22, 1865, George reported the welcome news of Lee's surrender to Grant:

We are having beautiful weather here at times within the last week, but it, like the Rebels, has been very treacherous of late. Perhaps capricious would be a better name for the many changes, but before long nature here will be dressed in her most lovely robes of beauty. Many trees are now in bloom and some of the forest trees begin to swell their buds, or rather unfold them to leaves. Last night we had a heavy thunder storm here, and the grass looks much greener for it.

We received the news of Lee's surrender here at about half past eleven last night, and at midnight a salute of some 30 guns was fired. You ought to have heard the bustle and noise in camp. Winchester has a kind of curious appearance just now, blue and gray uniforms mingle, apparently good friends, as several Rebel organizations have been disbanded near their place lately—there are a good number of the latter—they are coming in by squads to get paroles or take the oath, I don't know which. There is now not another Rebel organization existing in Virginia that I know of. Our business seems to have become to drill, have inspections and reviews. I hope that soon we will be sent home. Johnston, it seems, has not yet surrendered his Army, but we will hardly be called on to help fight any, should he determine to do so, as Sheridan's Cavalry can soon be with Sherman, and if he could not fight before, it would be madness for him to fight afterwards.

On April 30, 1865, George reflected to Kate on the shocking news of the assassination of President Lincoln:

> The assassination of the President was, as you may imagine, taken rather hard by the soldiers, for I believe that nowhere was he more loved and respected in the Army, and had the Rebels kept up resistance longer, scenes of violence and bloodshed might have followed that have not before been seen in this war, but most of the Rebels have been loud in denouncing the murderer, and our soldiers see the necessity for forbearance to the deceived of this country, to the continuance of the Republican form of Government based on union of the people.
>
> Our Chaplain's name is Collier. He is liked very well by some, but censored by others. Censored, as they say, for not preaching only the Gospel but mixing it with politics and sometimes laughable things. He, however, understands to win the soldiers, and many that thought him not much account at first admit now that he is a very good man.

In his May 3, 1865 letter, George reported from Winchester that a long march toward the West was being prepared:

> I will write a few lines this afternoon, as there are preparations going on now in three Regiments of our Brigade for a big march of somewhere. There have been no orders issued to us, but teamsters are being detailed today and the commissary has orders to have 25 days rations loaded. It is generally supposed that our route will be by Staunton and through the Kanawha Valley, but this, of course, is only supposition.
>
> Our pickets that went out this morning have been relieved again, and just came into camp. That looks as though we are going to start tomorrow morning. I almost dread a march of that kind, as it is nearly 300 miles to go the way that seems to be laid out for us.

In his May 23, 1865 letter from Staunton, Va., George regaled Kate with the amazing versatility of the students at the Romney school for its deaf, dumb and blind is a concert organized by the chaplains. The ability of deaf students to join in a chorus, plus their accurate knowledge of arithmetic, geography and other subjects was even more remarkable considering that the teacher was himself deaf and dumb.

> There was a sale of condemned U.S. property here yesterday, and I think is going on today. All of it is such, of course, as the now deceased Confederacy once laid claim to. The citizens about here had taken possession of it, but some of them soon brought in what they had and all of it will be gathered before long, as they are informing on each other.
>
> Citizens and soldiers are getting on quite intimate terms with each other. First they expressed their surprise about the good behavior and manly bearing of our troops as compared with Hunter's men (as they said) last year. But when they were told that the troops now here was a part of that very Army and the cause of the different behavior told them by the men, they hardly knew what to make of it, and many of them freely admit now they were deceived by ambitious but disappointed politicians. There are still some, however, who think that something will turn up to give the South her rights.
>
> One evening last week there was a concert (at the deaf and dumb and blind institute) given by the blind, assisted by the bands of this Brigade, for the benefit of the inmates, as there was nothing more to feed them with. Some of them came to the camps to beg for something to eat. There are about thirty of these unfortunates here at present. The concert was got up by the (our) Chaplains. I believe there was no tickets sold to citizens. $347.00 was the amount raised, at twenty-five cents each. The principal of the Institution then proposed to give an exhibition of the manner of teaching his pupils.
>
> We have nothing to do now but guard ourselves, and you will think after all this that soldiering is or must be real easy and

nice now, but this is not the case. There is more dissatisfaction now than ever there has been since we have been in the service. We have all sorts of rumors here, but as we get no news, we have nothing reliable. The latest paper that I have seen is the 15th. Staunton is a neat little city with nice front yards to most of the houses, filled with flowers and shrubbery, especially roses of red, white and yellow color.

There is a rumor just came through camp that we would stay here 30 days longer; of course, grape-vine as we call it.

I am well and hope this will find you enjoying good health. Give my love to all enquiring friends.

Has Father put his claim of brother John's back pay into the hands of any agent yet? If he has not, tell him to do so, but not pay them anything until after the claim is allowed.

Our Chaplains have had meetings in the Methodist or Baptist Church nearly every evening since we came here. The buildings, I think, were offered for use. There is a temperance society of over 500 in this Regiment now.

ABOUT ALL THAT GEORGE could report to Kate in his letter of June 11, 1865, was that he was still in Staunton, with "no prospect of getting away soon":

We are still in camp here at this place, with no prospect of getting away soon. The men that enlisted in this Regiment in '62 are ordered to be mustered out—no others as yet.

There is a sale to come off here on the 15th of Government property, to continue till all of the condemned property is sold. I do not think now that we will ever have that long march to make. There is a rumor that we will have to go to Lexington or Buchanan before long. Whether there is any truth in the report time will prove.

I hope to get home soon, but there is no prospect of it now, or any sign that I could tell by. Whenever you will see an order from the War Department to discharge veterans you may look for us home after a while, making due allowance for slow movements of all but the men concerned.

"Please do not get the blues if I don't make it home for a little while," was the only news that George could write Kate from Cumberland on June 26, 1865:

> I shall send a hundred dollar note in this. You had better put it into the bank for the present, for safe keeping.
>
> I am well and hope this will find you enjoying good health. God, who has so far preserved me, will not forsake me now. His will alone will be done.

In his final letter to Kate on July 7, 1865, from Wheeling, W.Va., George wrote he regrets that he and others have been placed on "regimental duty" and have had to wait further before getting discharged.

> My dear Sister:
>
> I will try and write a few lines to you, after being here for some time. When I wrote to you from Cumberland I did not expect that we would be put on duty again after being relieved at Staunton, and march to there, it being the rendezvous appointed by the War Department to muster out troops at, from the Department of West Virginia, but I and a good many others were disappointed in that, for part of the Regiment is now again on duty. Two Companies at Grafton, four at Wheeling in the City, and four Companies are camped here near town, not doing anything but regimental duty.
>
> I may get a pass next week and come down to Marietta for a few days, but I am not sure that I can.
>
> The cornerstone of a Soldier's Monument was laid here last Fourth, and the Governor dedicated for a Soldier's cemetery, on a hill near the City, in the forenoon. Afternoon there was several picnics near town. I was at one of them awhile but I did not stay very long.
>
> Have you received the money and papers I sent by Chaplain Collier? Perhaps you have had a chance now to see the man yourself and judge of him. What I wrote about him I wrote because I did not then wish to say any more, but I have since come to the

conclusion that as a Chaplain he is of but little account to the service. He tries to say smart things and keep on the good side of everybody. The consequence is he destroys his influence for good by all.

I am well and hope these few lines will find you enjoying good health.

Much love, from

Your brother, George

47. At War's End Hechler Returns to Marietta, then on to Dalton, Missouri

ONCE THE 36TH O.V.I. Regiment was mustered out on July 27, 1865 at Wheeling, West Virginia, they still had to travel to Columbus, Ohio, for final paperwork before being discharged. Cpl. Hechler returned to Marietta to rejoin his favorite sister Kate. He still found an uncomfortable relationship with his father, so he decided to move west to Missouri in 1866.

Earlier in 1866, on March 19 he appeared in Probate Court in Marietta to be sworn in as a citizen. His naturalization certificate states: "George Hechler proved to the satisfaction of the Court that he has resided in the United States for a least one year, that he has been honorably discharged from the Army of the United States and that he has behaved as a man of good moral character, attached to the principles of the Constitution of the United States, and well-disposed to the good order and happiness of the same, and having complied with the laws of the United States in relation to the Naturalization of Aliens."

On being admitted by the Court, he took the oath "to support the Constitution of the United States of America, and to Absolutely and Entirely Renounce and Adjure all allegiance and fidelity to every Foreign Prince, Potentate, State of Sovereignty Whatever, and particularly to Charles 1st, whose subject he was."

Later in 1866 he went to Missouri, settling in Sedalia.

On September 20, 1867, he enrolled in Rohrer's Commercial College located at 210 and 212 North 4th Street, St. Louis, Mis-

George Hechler, in retirement at Dalton, Mo.

souri, where he studied Double Entry Book-keeping, Commercial Calculation (Arithmetic), Commercial Penmanship, and Commercial Law. He was graduated on March 9th, 1868. Tuition paid in advance for the entire course was $70.00.

George Hechler went to Chariton County in March of 1868 and began working on Wm. H. Bitter's farm, southeast of Dalton. During the next seven years he also did farm work for Henry Meyer and other neighbors of Mr. Bitter.

On March 25, 1879, he married Mrs. Eliza Steiman whose husband had died January 22, 1875. Her maiden name was Sasse. She was born June 20, 1849 in Brunswick, Missouri. Her ancestors

Eliza Hechler, Dalton, Mo. 1908

were born in Germany. She and her parents moved to a farm southwest of Dalton when she was just a child. She was the daughter of Charles Sasse and Mary (Munson) Sasse. Her father, Charles Sasse went to Brunswick from Germany in 1842.

Mr. and Mrs. George Hechler lived on and operated a 387-acre livestock and grain farm south of Dalton, Bowling Green Township, until their retirement in 1915 when they moved to Dalton, Missouri, and rented their land to local farmers. They had about 100 head of cattle and hogs.

GEORGE HECHLER FAMILY RESIDENCE, DALTON, MO.

George Hechler was an active member of the Grand Army of the Republic, Rinehart Post, Brunswick, Missouri. He attended most of the National Annual G. A. R. Meetings held in different cities each year, as long as his health permitted.

He was confirmed and joined the Evangelical Lutheran Church in 1854. In 1890 he joined Immanuel Methodist Church, North, located 3 ¼ miles south of Dalton, serving as Sunday School teacher and Trustee of that church for several years.

He was well informed, a good thinker, and a conservative man of few words. While he was most tolerant, there never was any question where he stood on any moral question.

He was very much interested in Education, serving as Director and Clerk of his local School Board. He provided his three sons, Charles, George and Roy, with a good education. All were graduated from the University of Missouri at Columbia.

He took a most active interest in the progress of the Dalton Community and Chariton County, steadfastly supporting and working for all worthwhile programs of church, school, community and county.

He was one of the organizers of the Bank of Dalton and served on the Board of Directors a number of years.

After a long and useful life of 88 years and 10 months he passed away on August 17, 1929. Funeral services were held in the Dalton Methodist Church, with Reverends Schnackenberg and Mangold officiating.

Interment was in the Dalton Cemetery. Since there were only three surviving members of the Grand Army of the Republic's Rinehart Post, Brunswick's Rucker-McAllister Post of the American Legion graciously volunteered to pay final military honors by firing three volleys and sounding taps.

Index